Tamsin Simounds has written the book I wish had existed when I was busy confusing motion for progress. If you've ever ticked every box and still felt hollow, this book will help you understand why, and what to do next.

—Dom Price,
Work Futurist

As someone who's had a front row seat to Tamsin's remarkable, ever-evolving career, I came to this book with seriously high expectations—and it absolutely delivered. *The Experiment Mindset* offers practical, actionable ideas through engaging storytelling. It will remain on my bookshelf as a go-to handbook for years to come. I can't recommend it highly enough.

—Ben Avery,
Multi-award-winning Journalist

A thoroughly enjoyable book that is a must read for anyone who feels some version of 'stuck' in their life. Tamsin's voice is powerful, informative, funny and strengthened by the sharing of her own personal experiences throughout. *The Experiment Mindset* left me with a stack of handwritten notes in the margins and a new approach to life's challenges. Loved every word!

—Dr Michael Filosi,
Dentist, Business Leader and Entrepreneur

The EXPERIMENT MINDSET

The EXPERIMENT MINDSET

Unlocking the Science of **Personal Growth**

TAMSIN SIMOUNDS

WILEY

First published 2026 by John Wiley & Sons Australia, Ltd

The right of Tamsin Simounds to be identified as the author of *The Experiment Mindset* has been asserted in accordance with law.

ISBN: 978-1-394-38939-1

A catalogue record for this book is available from the National Library of Australia

Registered Office
John Wiley & Sons Australia, Ltd. Level 4, 600 Bourke Street, Melbourne, VIC 3000, Australia

For details of our global editorial offices, customer services, and more information about Wiley products visit us at www.wiley.com.

Wiley also publishes its books in a variety of electronic formats and by print-on-demand. Some content that appears in standard print versions of this book may not be available in other formats.

Author photo: Asher Milgate
Cover design by Wiley
Cover images: © Yuliya Chsherbakova/Shutterstock, © IrisImages/Getty Images

Set in 12/16.5pt and Adobe Garamond Pro by Straive, Chennai, India.

SKY10156025_050626

*To Flynn and Charlie.
May your lives be filled with wondrous adventures.*

Contents

Introduction   *xi*

Part I Understanding the science of personal
            growth   1

1   What keeps people stuck   3

2   The neuroscience of growth   19

3   Testing what works for you with the N-of-1 approach   33

Part II The three levers for growth   51

4   Environment   53

5   Physiology   69

6   Psychology   87

Part III The Experiment Mindset method   113

7   Designing your experiments   115

8   Translating information to wisdom   135

9   When experiments 'fail'   157

Part IV Living an experimental life   171

10   Minimising risk without losing momentum   173

11   The Experiment Mindset at work   187

12   Living experimentally   203

Conclusion   215

References and further reading   221

About the author   231

Acknowledgements   233

Introduction

The moment that reality finally smacked me in the face wasn't spectacular. It was a Tuesday afternoon in my kitchen and I'd spent the day trying to work from home with a baby who had very strong opinions about my output. The house was a mess, my inbox was overflowing and I had a big meeting looming that I hadn't prepared for. It was just after 4 pm and I found myself doing mental gymnastics with the clock, trying to decide when it became socially acceptable to pour a glass of red. I decided that time was now. I poured it.

A few minutes later, I heard a knock at the front door and panic surged.

No-one can see this.

It was my mother-in-law.

I tipped the wine down the sink, hid the glass in the dishwasher, brushed my teeth and opened the door with a smile that said, 'I'm fine. Everything's fine'. I invited her in and offered her a glass of wine. It was more acceptable to drink before 6 pm on a Tuesday with company, surely. We chatted and I played the part, but when she left I found myself back in the same spot, looking at the almost empty bottle on the bench.

I felt sick. I had just done exactly what I'd watched my dad do my whole life—drink the feelings, and then perform like everything was normal.

Standing there with a mix of wine and toothpaste on my breath and shame in my chest, I was transported back in time. I thought about the little girl with pigtails who used to say she wanted to be 'the boss' when she grew up. I was a little girl in a small South Australian country town so, as you can imagine, my statement was usually met with either a condescending pat on the head or a steer toward a more appropriate career, such as a teacher or a nurse.

The ups and downs of my career reality

I loved my rural upbringing and wouldn't trade it for city life, but in terms of exposure to what was possible, it was limited. When it came to choosing a career path, nothing set my soul on fire. I dabbled in a journalism degree, decided it wasn't for me, and then thought that since I had no idea what I wanted, I should just do a degree that would get me a 'good, solid job'. Go to work, get paid and go home. No big aspirations or special talents required. My dad went and got a chest x-ray one day and mentioned that the female radiographer was really nice and that he could see me doing something like that. So I did.

I finished my medical imaging degree and got my top choice of graduate jobs straight out of university. At my three-month review, they asked what I thought I'd specialise in. CT? MRI? Ultrasound? I said, 'I'm actually interested in what makes this business work. I think I want to move into management one day'.

I didn't know it at the time, but that comment set me on a fast track to leadership. Not much more than a year later, at the ripe old age of 24, I was running my first medical imaging clinic. A few years after that I was area manager of eight clinics across South Australia with a team of over 100 people and a multimillion-dollar budget, before eventually becoming organisational development manager for the company.

Living a life on repeat

At that point, I'd made my younger self proud. I was a 'boss'. But my life wasn't what I thought it would be. My health and my relationships were suffering as I tried to prove myself in these demanding roles, and I went to work every day waiting for the tap on the shoulder, that moment when someone would call me out and tell me I had no idea what I was doing. The big milestones I was ticking off—the promotions, the pay rises, the new house, the dream car—were exciting to chase, but the shine quickly wore off.

I'd watched my dad live his life the same way.

Growing up, my dad was wildly high functioning. He held senior roles in local government, coached local sport and was well known in our community. He was smart, immaculately presented, charming and capable. He supported me in the big stuff, including driving me to state basketball trials. When I was weighing up career options, he took me to meet politicians in Parliament House and introduced me to lawyers and journalists. He paid my rent when I moved to the city for uni. He wanted me to succeed.

But behind the scenes he was also deeply unwell.

He'd now tell you, in his own words, 'I wore a mask to hide my mental health and addiction issues'.

He'd come home from a successful day at work already holding a beer. I learned to dread the sound of another can opening. On the outside, we looked like the perfect family. On the inside, he was slowly unravelling, numbing a pain that achievement never managed to touch.

By the time I was in my early 30s, the performance had collapsed. He could no longer work, his relationships had broken down, and he'd cycled in and out of treatment and crisis so many times I'd lost count. It was devastating to watch, and the worst part was I couldn't do anything to stop it.

Looking back at the polished version of our life from the outside, the reality would have seemed impossible. But I'd watched it happen in slow motion.

Standing there in my kitchen, glass in the dishwasher and shame in my chest, I realised something that made my stomach turn. I wasn't just stressed; I was reliving his story. The thing that terrified me most wasn't that I might fail in my career. It was that I might succeed at building a life that would cause me to spiral in the same way.

Finding a new path

I didn't quit my job the next morning or flee to a villa in Bali to 'find myself'. I had a baby, a mortgage, a job and a family who depended on me. I didn't know how to step off the path I had built, but I knew I couldn't keep walking it the same way.

So I started testing new paths. At first, my experiments didn't look like experiments at all. They looked like late-night Google searches about psychology and behaviour change. They looked like saying yes to a leader-as-coach program instead of another management course, and like following that breadcrumb trail to a Diploma of Modern Psychology that required five weeks in Noosa and being in class six days a week, from 8 am until 6 pm.

That program didn't ask me and my fellow students to memorise frameworks and then try to remember them back at work. It asked us to lift ourselves out of our lives and test things on ourselves—on our patterns and on the stories we had built our lives around.

That was the first time I began to understand what this book is truly about. I started to understand the power of gathering experiences and data that change the story you tell yourself about who you are, and allow life to open up.

From there, the experiments grew but the principles stayed the same: try something, reflect, learn, adapt and evolve. Run a workshop, write an article, expand my network, learn to surf, travel alone, have a conversation, structure my week differently, say no to big opportunities that are actually distractions and say yes to opportunities I don't feel ready for. Learn what happens and continue.

My life certainly didn't become more predictable, but it did become more honest, more aligned and more mine.

That willingness to test, to try, to fail safely, to listen and to adapt became the foundation of everything I now teach and speak to audiences about—and, eventually, the foundation of this book.

As the experiments and learnings grew, I decided to launch my own coaching program, called Lead ID. I wanted to give people starting out in leadership the skills, self-awareness and support I wished I'd had in the early days. The program was more successful than I expected. Over the nine years since starting Lead ID, I've coached hundreds of leaders, emerging leaders, CEOs, professional athletes and high-growth founders. I've spoken on stages across Australia and worked with some of our most recognised brands to help them build cultures where the organisation, the human, the income and the impact can all grow together.

On paper, my journey looks pretty linear, but it certainly didn't feel that way. My career reality has been closer to that shown in the following figure.

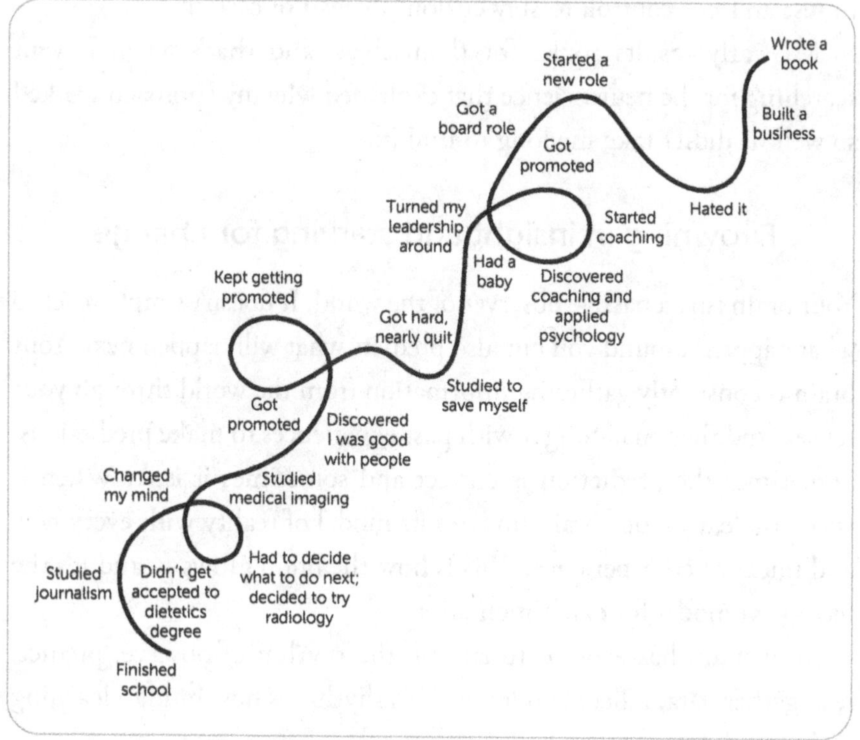

My non-linear career journey

Understanding the Experiment Mindset

What I'm sharing with you in this book isn't theory I studied and decided to teach. It's a framework I've built from almost two decades of lived leadership experience, a lifetime of personal experience, a decade coaching hundreds of leaders and speaking to thousands, and extensive study across health science, modern psychology and neuroscience.

The more I worked with my clients, the more I noticed a pattern. The people who transformed most weren't the smartest or the most disciplined; they were the ones courageous enough to test something new. The same words came out of my mouth over and over again: 'You're either going to succeed or learn. It's just a data-gathering exercise'. I was using what I now call the Experiment Mindset — teaching clients how to test and not control; to stay curious instead of certain.

My early results spoke for themselves, and that's when I went searching for the neuroscience that explained why my approach worked so well. It didn't take me long to find it.

Drowning in insight and starving for change

Your brain isn't a passive observer of the world. It doesn't simply react to what happens around you but also predicts what will happen next. Your brain is constantly gathering information from the world through your senses, and then matching it with past experiences to make predictions. Sometimes the prediction is correct and sometimes it isn't. When it isn't, you learn. Your brain updates its model of reality with every new and unexpected experience. This is how the brain grows — and it's the biological model for experimentation.

Your brain has evolved to run on the rhythm of observe, predict, test, gather data, reflect and learn. This rhythm is how human learning and growth happen.

But most people are now doing the opposite. They're trying to control outcomes and cling to certainty. If something doesn't go to plan or is a bit ambiguous, we too often freak out, judge ourselves, feel bad and retreat to what's familiar, leaving us anxious, perfectionistic and stuck as a result.

If this sounds familiar, you're not alone. We're living in an age obsessed with improvement, where everywhere you look someone's offering a promise of a better version of yourself—slightly more refined, more regulated, more productive and more centred. We're chasing a protein-eating, early-rising, boundary-holding, ice-bathing, breath-working, spiritually awakened, habit-stacked, insight-soaked version of ourselves that, apparently, should be thriving by now.

The shelves are overflowing, the podcasts never end and half-finished online courses sit abandoned across the world, waiting for the moment we finally 'get serious'. And we keep buying.

Last year alone, according to consulting firm Grand View Research the global personal development industry generated more than $48 billion. If transformation could be purchased, and if clarity, confidence or self-worth came bundled in modules, we would be the most fulfilled and grounded generation in history. And, yet, we're not.

Despite all the information, tools and well-intentioned efforts to 'work on ourselves', the data tells a different story. People are more overwhelmed, more pressured, more burnt out and more uncertain about their direction than ever before. As shown in the following figure, as global spending on personal development has increased, according to Grand View Research's *Personal Development Market (2025–2030)*, the percentage of workers in Australia who say they are thriving has sharply dropped, according to Gallup's *State of the Global Workplace 2025* report.

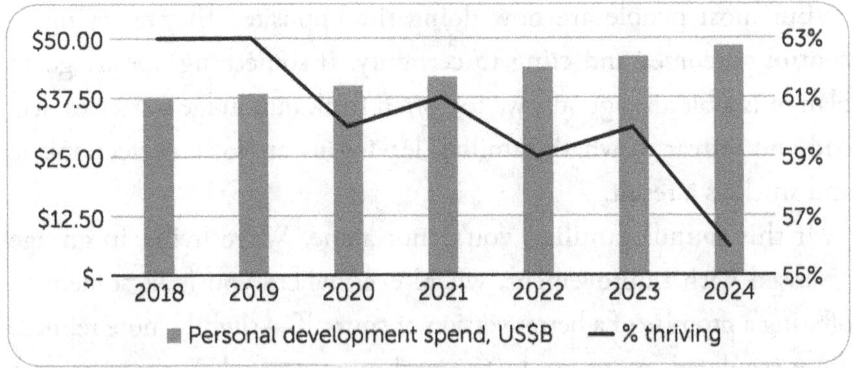

Personal development spending is up, while thriving is down

We are drowning in insight and starving for change.

This lack of progress or change isn't because we're lazy, or because we're undisciplined or fundamentally flawed. It's because we've built an entire industry around consuming information about change and almost nothing around the systems that help us turn information into lived, repeatable transformation. Somewhere along the way, we've fundamentally misunderstood what growth actually is.

Understanding how growth happens

You're not broken, and this book isn't about fixing you. It's about understanding how humans actually grow—biologically, psychologically and behaviourally—and how you can use that science to shape a life that feels aligned, energising and deeply your own. This is what I've discovered:

- Your brain doesn't change through wishing.
- Your identity doesn't change through thinking.
- Your confidence doesn't change through planning.
- Your life doesn't change through consuming more insight.
- You change through experimentation.

The Experiment Mindset I outline in this book offers a sense of freedom from the dominant script. It provides the opportunity to replace control with curiosity and perfectionism with play. It reminds you that the real work of growth is not to control outcomes but to run experiments that help you learn. When you start living experimentally, growth stops being something you chase and starts becoming something you create.

In the pages that follow, you'll learn how to move before you're ready, to learn as you go and to build a life that evolves with you instead of leaving you behind.

I'll help you make the seven fundamental shifts in how you approach your own growth shown in the following figure.

Traditional approach		Experiment Mindset
Goal setting	$\longrightarrow$	Horizon setting
Fixed identity	$\longrightarrow$	Evolving identity
Information	$\longrightarrow$	Wisdom
Control	$\longrightarrow$	Curiosity
Fixing what hurts	$\longrightarrow$	Changing what matters
Failure	$\longrightarrow$	Data
Fear	$\longrightarrow$	Freedom

Shifting how you approach growth

In the following chapters, I show you how to work with your whole system — your psychology, your physiology and your environment — so you're not fighting against parts of yourself while trying to force change in others. I help you design experiments, track what matters, respond to feedback and iterate your way toward a life that's actually yours.

This book isn't a map that points you toward the 'right' path — there is no such thing. Instead, this book outlines a method that teaches you how to walk your own path, gather data from your life, stay connected to who you're becoming and build your next chapter one experiment at a time.

You don't need certainty before you take the first step. You don't need a five-year plan. You don't need a deep understanding of who you are. And you don't need to feel fearless or ready or fully healed.

You just need a starting point and an experiment.

Let's begin.

PART I
Understanding the science of personal growth

Personal growth is not rocket science and you know it. By now you've likely read the books and listened to the podcasts. Maybe you've even done a few courses and hired a coach. You've got all the knowledge you need to change your life, find fulfilment and live up to your full potential. But you've bought another book.

In the coming chapters, I help you understand why that gap between what you know and what you're doing exists. I explore why the people who look most 'together' from the outside often feel the most stuck, how we confuse progress with growth and why knowledge alone never changes anything. I also run through what actually has to happen in your brain for real transformation to take root, and why what works for someone else might do nothing for you.

Most importantly, I show you how to treat your life like a laboratory instead of a performance review, using feedback and data, not people-pleasing and perfectionism, to design a life that actually works for you.

Remember—growth doesn't happen from having all the answers; it comes from running better experiments.

Ready?

1

What keeps people stuck

The message from Emma landed in my LinkedIn inbox late on a Friday night. 'I haven't done anything like this before and I don't even know if this is what I need, but I think I need to talk to someone. Can we book a session?'

I clicked through to Emma's profile. Viewed from the outside, Emma looked like a walking success story. She was a senior education-sector executive leading an influential government department. She had an executive title, which was undoubtedly attached to a healthy pay packet, and her profile photo showed a polished and professional woman in her late 40s — the type who looked like she had her shit together.

The picture didn't lie — that's exactly who walked into my office a few weeks later. Emma was polished but warm. She didn't dress in your typical corporate costume, and instead her outfit gave a gentle nod in the direction of 'I work in corporate, but at heart I'm a hippie'. She had a large, deep-green leather handbag, and put together hair that had seen a salon recently. She had it going on, but her eyes told a different story. You know when you can just see the lump in someone's throat?

We sat down and I waited.

'I don't know why I'm here', she said. Then she laughed. 'That's not true. I know exactly why I'm here. I just don't know how to say it without sounding ridiculous and ungrateful. Or crying.'

Emma started where most of my clients start. She listed her achievements like she was running through her credentials at a job interview, telling me about how she was the first in her family to go to university, completing a teaching degree she paid for herself. She described how she climbed steadily through the management ranks, becoming a department head, then executive director and now senior executive, leading policy that affected thousands of people and earning a salary that would have made her younger self incredibly proud.

'I keep getting tapped on the shoulder for my next opportunities, and that's been happening my whole career. I'm really thankful for that.' I saw her wince before getting the next bit out. 'But I don't know if I want this. I don't know what comes next. What's it all for?' And then the tears came, something I've come to witness over and over again in my office, combined with the relief of spilling the truth.

Emma wasn't stuck through lack of options. She had plenty. Other departments were already circling, wanting her expertise. She could take a sideways step into a different portfolio, or go for the next promotion, move to a bigger office with a better view and hang with the big wigs.

The beautiful but painful words that came next were the ones that made me lean forward in my seat. 'When I look at what's next, it all feels like more of the same—just different labels on the same doors. And I'm starting to wonder if I've been walking down the wrong corridor this whole time.'

Emma came from nothing. She was raised by a single mother who worked two jobs and still struggled to pay the bills. At school, while other kids were figuring out who to sit with at lunch, Emma was figuring out how to get out. She was going to make something of herself. She was going to earn enough money that she'd never have to count coins for groceries or put off the dentist or choose between electricity and rent.

And she did it. She worked her way through university, and because failure wasn't an option, she worked so hard that she excelled. She was great at her job, known as the type who would always go above and beyond, and so she got promoted over and over again. She was smart and reliable and innately knew how to get stuff done, lead a team and influence people, so she kept climbing. Every rung on that ladder felt like proof that she was doing it right, and every promotion felt like the security the little girl in Emma had always dreamed of.

'I thought if I could just get here, I'd feel different', she said. 'Settled. Like I'd arrived somewhere. But I don't feel settled. I feel trapped.'

At this point, however, Emma started listing barriers to getting out of this trap like she was ticking boxes on a form. 'I only know education.' 'I can't move states; my mum needs care.' 'I need this salary. I've got a mortgage and school fees to pay.' 'And even if I wanted to change, I wouldn't know where to start.'

Her future looked like a corridor of identical doors, each one leading to a slightly different version of the same life. She was being offered more responsibility, more pressure and more money to keep the life she'd built, but she wasn't sure she wanted anymore.

She was moving forward, but was she inspired? No.

This is where most people get stuck—not because they're lazy or lack ambition, but because they've confused progress with growth.

Progress ≠ growth

Progress and growth are not the same thing. Progress is forward movement toward a predetermined destination. Growth is the ongoing evolution of who you are. Progress looks like climbing the ladder, ticking the boxes and hitting the targets. It's measurable, linear and often external. You can point to it on a resume and it looks schmick. Growth feels aligned with your values and vision for your life. It's not about arriving somewhere, but becoming someone. Growth shifts your identity, rather than just your job title.

Growth and progress can overlap, and sometimes progress leads to growth. But the trap to look out for is that sometimes progress can disguise itself as growth so cleverly that you don't notice you're moving toward something you don't actually want.

Promotions feel like growth. Pay rises feel like growth. Ticking the next box feels like growth. But too often they're really just forward motion along a path you were too busy to question. This is compounded by the fact that everything around you is designed to keep you on that path. SMART goals, five-year plans, KPIs and your yearly performance review all aim to keep your eyes locked on a finish line.

You might have felt that creeping 'is that it?' feeling yourself. Maybe it drifts in after landing your dream job, finishing the marathon you'd been training hard for, buying the new car or moving into your ideal house. You get a brief high, and then the pressure to set the next goal kicks in before you've even caught your breath.

What you're feeling isn't just in your head, and you're certainly not alone.

Decades of research (for example, a study led by Joanne Dickson and published in *Psychiatry Research*) show that when your goals are tied to external markers such as titles, income or status, you're more likely to feel anxious while chasing them. Not only that but when you succeed, the satisfaction doesn't stick around. The cycle starts again, and you're back on the treadmill.

Reverting to your set point

Psychologists call this the 'hedonic set point'. Your brain has a baseline level of happiness, and it's remarkably stubborn. As shown in the following figure, positive or negative events such as promotions, break-ups, new relationships and setbacks can all shift the needle of overall happiness temporarily but, before you know it, you settle back to where you started—your brain's baseline for happiness.

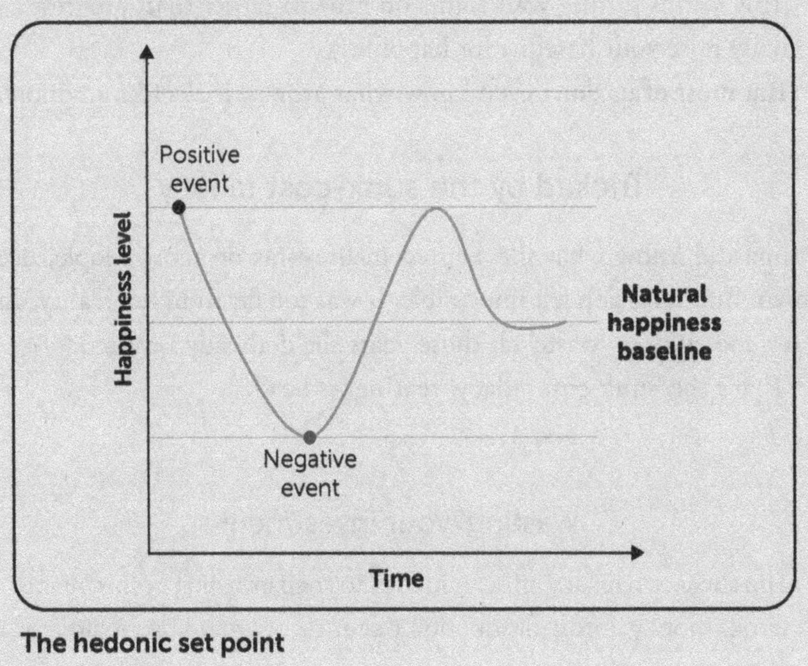

The hedonic set point

This is what was happening to Emma. She'd get a promotion and experience a temporary high of being chosen, and then she'd return to her baseline, wondering why it didn't feel as good as she thought it would.

Thankfully, you're not doomed to bounce back to your own base level for evermore, and you can actually raise your set point. A long-term study by Bruce Headey (published in *Social Indicators Research*) showed that goals with no end game—the kind related to how you want to feel, who you want to spend time with and the difference you want to make in the world—can raise your baseline level of happiness. But extrinsic goals, such as chasing career success and material wealth, keep you locked wherever you were genetically and environmentally set to land.

This means setting your sights on growth rather than progress can actually raise your baseline for happiness.

But most of us don't even know what growth looks like anymore.

Tricked by the sunk-cost fallacy

Emma did know what she wanted in life—as do most people, deep down. But the vision felt impossible. It was too far from her reality, and it felt too risky to 'waste' all those years she'd already invested.

That's the 'sunk-cost fallacy' rearing its head.

'Wasting' your investment

The sunk-cost fallacy is the tendency to keep investing in something (time, money, effort or identity) because of what you've already spent, even when it no longer serves you. This fallacy is why:

- people stay in jobs they hate (because 'I've already put ten years into this career')
- people finish degrees that no longer fit (because 'I'm already halfway through')

- ◆ people remain in relationships (because 'We've been together for five years')
- ◆ work projects continue even after they've become disasters (because 'We've already spent $2 million on this').

The sunk-cost fallacy tricks you into thinking that the investment you've already made is a reason to keep going. But, I'm sorry to tell you my friend, that investment is gone regardless of what you do next.

The question you need to ask yourself is this: 'If I hadn't already invested all this time, money and identity, would I choose this again today?'

For Emma, the sunk costs felt huge. They included her entire career path, her reputation, her professional network and decades of time. Every rung she'd climbed made it harder to imagine stepping sideways, let alone stepping off the ladder entirely.

Sometimes taking in the scale of change required feels too overwhelming to even entertain, so we look away. We tell ourselves it's not the right time, that we should be grateful, that other people have it worse. By the time we're ready to do it, we're looking back and it's too late.

I didn't ask Emma to blow up her life. I didn't ask her to quit her job or make any dramatic declarations. I asked her to take one small step and conduct one tiny experiment. This single action, approached with the mindset of a curious scientist, would eventually compound and change her trajectory. That's the power of compounding, and you'll see it again and again through this book.

Caught in the success trap

Emma's story isn't unique. I've seen it across hundreds of leaders. You might not be an education executive, but you likely know the feeling. You've followed the rules, ticked the boxes, made the 'smart' choices, and somehow still ended up stuck.

I've worked with an Australian Olympic volleyball prodigy. She focused her whole life on making it to the Olympics, only to arrive and wonder 'what's next?'

Another client, Cara, grew a business in the care sector. She went from thinking she was incapable and unemployable to building a seven-figure business. Once she'd done it, she started rolling up to work on a Monday with a pit in her stomach. She enjoyed the growth phase of the business and had expected to enjoy settling in for the ride once things were stable, but she felt restless.

On the surface, these people were wildly successful. Underneath, they were stuck in the same trap.

Counterintuitively, it is often the high performers who find themselves in this success trap the most. When you are used to succeeding, failure feels more than uncomfortable; it feels like a threat to who you are. Your brain has learned that achievement equals safety, approval and self-worth, so it becomes very good at steering you away from anything that might put that at risk.

Motivation scientist Professor Ayelet Fishbach, one of the world's leading researchers on human motivation, has shown in her work that people gravitate toward goals in areas they already feel competent. When something makes us feel skilled, effective or recognised, we want to stay there because competence feels safe and good.

In her book *Get It Done*, Fishbach explains that people often repeat behaviours that have worked before, even when those behaviours no longer support growth. Success reinforces the familiar, protecting our identity and making us surprisingly cautious about stepping into anything where we might look like a beginner again.

If your identity is wrapped up in being the reliable one, the smart one or the successful one, your brain will keep nudging you toward the familiar path where you know how to win, even if that path is draining the life out of you. You become exceptional at rationalising. You tell yourself it is not the right time to change, that you should be grateful, that it's silly to change it up now, and that other people have it worse. On the surface, you've nailed the performance, and you look driven and committed. Underneath, you are stuck.

You've built a life around being good at things, and stepping into something you might be bad at feels like a kind of ego death.

This isn't unfamiliar to me. I've been trying to win at everything since being exceptional at colouring inside the lines. I've chased jobs, and even boyfriends, that deep down I didn't really want, just because I wanted to prove I could have them. I was promoted every couple of years in my first real job, managing a team of over 100 and a multimillion-dollar budget, training in my free time for triathlons, sometimes twice per day. I was busting my butt, looking for my next win, waiting and searching for the moment I'd feel like I'd actually made it—like I was finally good enough and the success would hit deep enough.

That moment never came.

The myth of linear growth

We've been programmed to believe that success follows a straight line:

- Study hard, get good grades, land a good job, work your way up, achieve your goals and be happy.
- Choose a fitness plan, stick to it religiously, see consistent progress, reach your target weight and maintain it forever.
- Find the right person, fall in love, get married, have kids and live happily ever after.

But that's not how growth actually works. That's not how life works. And it's certainly not how careers work anymore.

The most successful people I know, the ones who find fulfilment in their work, who have meaningful relationships, who are making their mark on the world, who have grown and are growing, all share one thing in common. Their stories are just as winding, just as unpredictable and just as 'off track' as mine. This isn't an anomaly. It's how growth is meant to look.

Too often, we're obsessed with straight lines. In business, we call it scaling. In fitness, we track consistent progress. In careers, we want an upward trajectory. But actually ask anyone who has achieved something great? They'll tell you their growth looks nothing like a straight line.

Even your brain doesn't learn in straight lines. When you try to master something new, whether it's a language, a skill or a way of thinking, you experience periods of rapid improvement, followed by plateaus where progress seems to stall, and then sudden breakthroughs that can seem to emerge from nowhere. This isn't a bug in the system but how the system works. The straight-line climb might have worked in a more predictable world. But that's not the world we're living in.

I work with organisations all over Australia, and I can almost guarantee what happens when I ask to see their current strategy document to give me some insight into the direction they need their team to align toward. If this document is more than two years old, they hand it to me with the same heads-up: 'A lot of this has changed now. It's not really accurate anymore'.

One organisation I worked with was changing so rapidly that, over 18 months, I watched three major projects get launched and then shut down before they saw the light of day. An entire division was restructured out of existence. People who had spent years developing expertise in specific areas found their knowledge obsolete almost overnight. This wasn't a failing company. They were adapting to a world that is now changing faster than five-year plans can accommodate.

The way we approach our careers has also dramatically changed. In my parents' era, it was normal to progress through your career linearly within the confines of one or two organisations. My dad had a 40-year career in local government. Success within those careers was measured by promotions and salary raises.

Now? Traditional careers are quickly being replaced with what have become known as 'portfolio careers', with almost half of people aged between 18 and 43 earning their money from multiple sources.

The job title 'social media manager' didn't exist 20 years ago. 'Data scientist' was coined in 2008. 'App developer' became a career path only after 2009. According to recent *Forbes* article by Joe McKendrick on the impact of AI, around 40 years ago any new career skill you picked up had a half-life of at least ten years. Now? That's shrunk to about four years, and it's continuing to shrink rapidly.

The World Economic Forum's *Future of Jobs Report 2025* lists creative thinking, resilience, flexibility and agility, and curiosity and lifelong learning in the top six skills on the rise over the next five years. Yet we're still using strategic planning, goal setting and career frameworks designed for the industrial age, when careers followed predictable ladders and industries remained stable for decades. We're trying to plan five years ahead in a world where five months is ambitious, and that mismatch is making us miserable.

Straight-line anxiety

Here's what happens when you force linear progress in a non-linear world:

- You over-curate and overthink to avoid ambiguity.
- Goals feel overwhelming, triggering self-doubt or imposter syndrome.

- You chase productivity for its own sake.
- You compare your messy reality to everyone else's highlight reels.
- You feel competitive, even about things you don't want.
- You take the obvious next step and wonder why it feels flat.

Social media hasn't just given us more to compare ourselves to; it's made growth feel exposed. It can make you feel like every awkward phase, every experiment and every half-formed idea is happening in a human fishbowl, on display for everyone to see and judge.

That's enough to take us from discomfort to paralysis, while we ruminate on the age-old question: *But what will people think?*

I can practically see these words etched at the forefront of the minds of the people I work with who are about to take a brave step. Wouldn't it be nice to fast-forward to the success story at the end—where you're on Instagram talking about your successful business launch or five-star review, showing off your fit new bod or flashing your Strava stats of the marathon you just ran?

Baring the messy middle bit, where you just don't know what's about to happen, isn't as easy. And if you're deviating off track, it's normal to think people might look at you and question 'what are they doing?'

It's normal for that to grip at your insides. You care because you're wired that way. Human beings are social creatures who for hundreds of thousands of years have needed to belong to survive. Your nervous system knows how important it is to stay with the tribe, so it treats your potential judgement like a physical threat. Of course you feel exposed when you step onto a path that doesn't make immediate sense to other people. It's kind of like stepping out solo into open grasslands in the African savanna and screaming, 'Here lions, come at me!' You're going to hesitate. It's not wrong to feel this way; it's normal.

But I can offer a workaround.

Living experimentally means shifting your reference point from performing for whoever's watching, to performing for the person you're becoming—for your future self and the version of you who actually reaps the reward.

It's also important to remember that most people aren't watching as closely as you think, and the people who are will judge you anyway. You'll get opinions if you stay where you are. You'll get opinions if you grow. You don't get the luxury of avoiding judgement and only get to choose what you're judged for. You might as well make the show interesting.

Most people sit safely on the sidelines, offering commentary. Very few step out onto the field where the work actually happens—where it's hot and uncomfortable and uncertain and completely worth it. That's where you grow.

You can't live an experimental life while editing yourself for spectators. At some point you have to choose between their comfort and your direction.

Escaping the trap

You can see why people stay stuck, and it's hard to blame them. It's no wonder we're consuming more personal development content than ever before. We want out, but we don't know how.

Emma's story out didn't go the way you might expect.

She didn't quit her job, and she didn't make a dramatic career pivot, start a new degree or take on a non-profit board role. She didn't even start with a work experiment.

It turned out that what Emma was looking for in her career—joy, freedom, excitement and meaning—was actually missing in her life outside of work. Her job had become the place she was trying to get all her needs met, and no job, no matter how good, can do that.

This meant her first experiment wasn't professional but personal. She started painting again, something she'd given up when she became a manager 20 years ago. Every Sunday morning, before her family woke up, she'd set herself up in the spare room and paint for a couple of hours. She had no end game in mind or big goal. Her aim was just to paint. It reminded her of who she was, and that her life extended beyond work.

Then she reconnected with old friends, people she'd lost touch with during the climb, or people she'd connected with and said, 'We must catch up some time' and then never did. She found time for coffee dates, long walks and conversations that had nothing to do with education policy or departmental budgets.

And as her reconnection with herself continued, the realisation came. She ended a relationship that had run its course. I won't share the details, they're hers. But I watched her come to life in a way she never had when we talked about work.

This growth wasn't how Emma expected things to unfold. It's not even how I expected them to unfold. When she started painting, she wasn't trying to fix her relationship or trying to find clarity. She was just painting. The path wasn't clear until she was walking on it, and the change didn't happen until she was in it.

That's the thing about these life experiments: you can't see around the corner from where you're standing. You have to take the step first. Clarity comes through the doing, not before it.

Over time, Emma stopped putting pressure on her job to bring her back to life, and the life returned to her work. We're two years down the track as I write this, and her personal life has transformed in ways she didn't see coming. She's still in her old job, and she loves it.

'I couldn't think of a better role for myself right now', she told me recently. 'It's meaningful, impactful and it uses all my strengths. The difference is I'm not asking it to be my entire life anymore.'

She's turned down four different promotions and career opportunities in the past two years, not because she's scared or stuck, but because she knows what she wants and, more importantly, she knows what she doesn't. She can enjoy her work now because she's not putting pressure on it to fill every hole in her life. She found what was missing, just not where she expected to find it.

This is the wonder and beauty of non-linear growth. You can only join the dots backward, never in a straight line forward. Emma couldn't have planned her growth; instead, she had to live into it. But whatever the trajectory, she's on track, because she designed it that way. She's grown, but she hasn't climbed.

That's what you're about to learn how to do — not by mapping out the perfect five-year plan, but by understanding how your brain actually changes, what conditions it needs to grow and how to run small experiments that compound into transformation.

You don't need to blow up your life. You just need to set your compass to true north and start experimenting toward it. The Experiment Mindset works because your brain was built to grow like this.

Let's get into how.

Reflection prompts

◆ What are you continuing to do primarily because of what you've already invested? If you hadn't already spent all that time, money, effort or identity, would you choose it again today?

◆ Where have you confused progress with growth?

2

The neuroscience of growth

One of the best (and seemingly productive) procrastination methods you'll ever see from someone who wants to grow is picking up a book. Maybe that's you right now. And, look, worse vices exist than reading. But if you've ever plugged into the podcasts, had books piling up on your bedside table, binged on personal development content and still found yourself wondering why you're not actually changing, you'll know what I mean.

With a lens of self-compassion, this approach makes sense. Wanting to learn more is a noble pursuit. But learning about growth isn't the same thing as growing. This is because growth, both in your brain and in your life, isn't learned. It's trained.

Growth isn't learned but trained

Growth doesn't come from hoarding information; it comes from gathering experience. That's how your brain works. Psychologist and neuroscientist Lisa Feldman Barrett's groundbreaking work on emotions has shown that your brain isn't just passively meeting a moment and reacting. It's predicting what's going to happen before it happens, matching information from the environment with your own prior experiences, acting accordingly, and then updating future predictions based on what unfolds.

Think of your brain as being similar to the autocomplete on your phone, always trying to guess the next word. Most of the time it gets it right; however, when it doesn't, you notice.

This process is your brain's way of adapting to its environment. To conserve energy, it doesn't process every scrap of data from the world around you, because that would be overwhelming. Instead, it filters for what matches its predictions, and it pays special attention to what doesn't. That's why sudden loud noises grab your attention, and why things that are novel pique your interest. These moments where reality doesn't line up with what your brain thought was coming next are called prediction errors, and this is a similar process to what you're working with when you run experiments. You build a hypothesis (predictions), act accordingly, take in the data, reflect, learn and adapt. Experiments work within the same patterns already used by your brain. That's what makes them so powerful.

Imagine you're a nervous public speaker and you're invited to sit on a panel. Usually you'd decline the offer, but you want to grow into public speaking so you decide to run an experiment and test the following hypothesis: 'I'll test taking on more public speaking opportunities for six months to learn if it builds my confidence and begins to feel less scary'. You show up for the panel, and you survive it. You actually think you might have done pretty well! Where in the past you may have predicted, 'I'll freeze, I'll forget my words and I'll make a fool of myself', you now have fresh evidence that challenges that old operating model. The more you do it, the stronger this evidence gets.

You're predicting the future based on your past experiences. But every time you add a new experience, you're updating your prediction machine. You're growing—literally.

Understanding the plasticity of your brain

For thousands of years, before modern neuroscience even existed, we understood that the brain can change—albeit with great difficulty, persistence, and a whole lot of time and patience. A concept attributed to Roman poet Ovid (and then later expanded) captures the belief of his time perfectly: 'Gutta cavat lapidem non vi sed saepe cadendo', which translates as 'A water drop hollows a stone, not by force, but by falling often'. Up until relatively recently, this continued to be how we thought change worked. Your brain was essentially fixed, carved in stone, and transformation required the painfully slow, patient work of water dripping over decades.

Eventually we upgraded our metaphor using the idea that our brain was wired, more like a computer. Some limited rewiring might be possible, but still your basic operating system was installed during early childhood, and from around the age of 25 it was mostly permanent.

Now, through modern neuroscience, we understand that your brain can and does change—yes, during childhood, but even into old age. It is adaptable, mouldable and constantly reshaping itself in response to experience. Neuroscientists refer to this feature as *neuroplasticity*—the brain's ability to form and reorganise neural connections, especially in response to experience. Your brain can change, adapt and rewire itself throughout your entire life. You really can teach an old dog new tricks.

This means a better metaphor is to think of your brain as a living forest. Your embedded ways of thinking, feeling and operating are like well-trodden and smooth paths through this forest. The paths less travelled are so overgrown they're barely visible. When you experience something new, find a new perspective or choose to respond with a different emotion, you're essentially carving a new pathway. If you continually do that, with the right conditions, your brain starts to use this pathway more, and this new way of thinking, being or doing becomes embedded in your default operating system like a well-lit highway. The path you used to use gets used less and less, and it starts to weaken, becoming more like an overgrown off-road hiking trail.

Just because your brain can change, doesn't mean it will

I first learnt about the brain's ability to change a decade ago, before I'd done much study on brain science other than some basic anatomy during my medical imaging degree. I naively believed that, armed with this new understanding about how our brains worked, 'humans overall would suddenly be more likely to change—due to some kind of neuroscience-sparked revolution. But, of course, that wasn't the case.

A magical wave of transformation didn't occur when neuroplasticity hit the mainstream. People didn't suddenly start becoming the versions of themselves they actually wanted to be. Why not? Because knowing your brain can change and actually creating the conditions for that change to happen are two completely different things.

The end of history illusion

The fact that change is possible is broadly understood now. Yet, how often have you heard, or maybe even said, something along the lines of, 'This is just who I am'?

Psychologists call this the 'end of history illusion'. In 2013, Jordi Quoidbach, Daniel Gilbert, and Timothy Wilson published the results of their study of almost 20 000 people aged 18 to 68. The study had asked participants to report on how much they had changed in the past decade, and then to predict how much they thought they would change in the next ten years. No matter their age, young, old or in between, participants believed they had changed a lot in the past, but likely wouldn't change much in the future.

In other words, people believe that who they are today is pretty much who they will be tomorrow, despite the fact that it isn't who they were yesterday. This end of history illusion has the inevitable consequence of limiting our future opportunities for growth while we double-down on our current approach to life. This might not too bad if your current approach is working for you, but it does beg the question: what else is possible?

I can remember standing in the viewing room of the x-ray department I was working in, surrounded by the bright white light of the viewing boxes. I was chatting to a colleague, who was also an old university friend, and I said, 'I'll never be one of those people who loves what they do. I was always envious of those people who knew what they wanted to be when they grew up'. I wasn't yet 30, and I thought any possibility of change was all over for me.

I'd followed the path I'd always known. It was so familiar and well worn that I thought it was set in stone. The path of working hard, getting good grades, getting promoted, saying yes and keeping climbing was etched in my identity. 'This is just who I am.'

My brain had become like a forest with pathways used so repeatedly they might as well have been bituminised. The path I'd been taking—that of the relentless achiever driven to compete to win, even for things I didn't really want—had been travelled so many times that it felt like the only way through. It was wide and clear, and I could walk it with my eyes closed.

But countless other pathways were possible in that forest. Some were overgrown from years of neglect, while others were completely hidden, waiting to be discovered.

The problem is, the process of going off track is really energy taxing.

The energetic cost of change

Your brain is a complex organ, tasked with the important job of keeping you alive. It works through communication between nerve cells—neural pathways—which transmit information to and from the body. While your brain only accounts for around 2 per cent of your total body weight, it saps up around 25 per cent of your entire energy usage each day. You might be keen to use that energy to grow toward your full potential, but your brain couldn't care less. Its priority is to keep your heart beating, and to keep you safe, fed and comfortable, and it'll conserve as much energy as it can to do so. Your brain may be plastic, but first and foremost it's efficient. Anything automatic, such as your usual habits, routines and predictions, are metabolically cheaper and, therefore, preferred over more taxing tasks. And what are your most energy-expensive activities? Moving your body, learning new things and navigating uncertainty.

You can see why you need to work with your brain, not against it.

Creating the conditions for growth

Until the age of around 25, neuroplasticity occurs pretty easily and organically through passive experience. A young child's nervous system is geared for change — and it wants to change. At this early age, simply engaging with the natural world, such as staring out into the garden and watching an insect float down and land on a flower unexpectedly, is enough to set the brain alight and build new pathways. As we get older, though, neuroplasticity is less passive.

Unfortunately, you can't just decide to change your brain and pop out the other side as a brand new human. You need to go through a series of steps, a process, in order to get yourself into a state that makes change more likely to occur. If you create the right circumstances in your brain — including the right chemistry, the right environment and the right perspective — your nervous system will arrive in a state in which change isn't just possible but also likely. This process forms the foundation of the Experiment Mindset.

Self-directed neuroplasticity

Neuroplasticity in itself is simply a brain trait that has evolved to help us adapt to our environments and survive. In the area of personal growth, the focus is on harnessing this ability to realise your own potential. To do so, you need to establish the conditions required to rewire your brain in line with the direction you want to go, take action, usually against some resistance, and have some time to rest and reflect.

As shown in the following figure, this process of 'self-directed neuroplasticity has four steps: awareness, focused experience, reflection and consolidation.

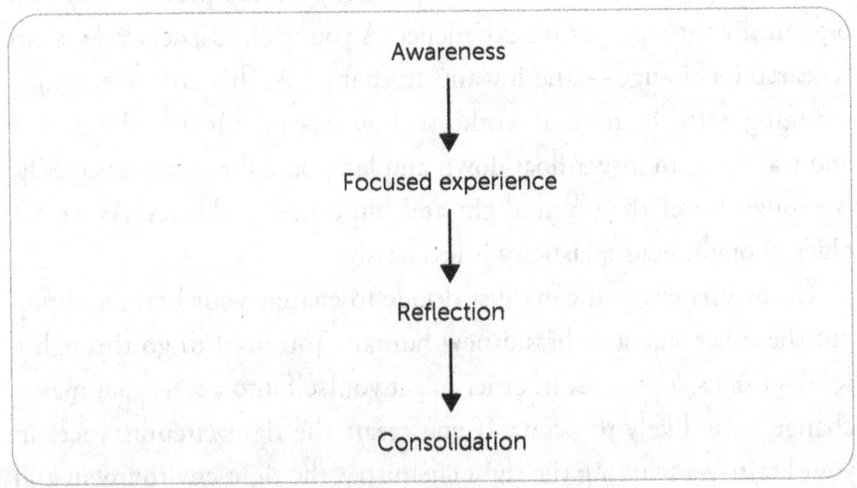

The self-directed neuroplasticity process

The following sections expand on each of these four steps.

Awareness

I had just turned 29 when I married my husband. Our honeymoon was an incredible adventure driving a campervan around the South Island of New Zealand, followed by some relaxation in the paradise island of Aitutaki in the Cook Islands. The road trip allowed for plenty of conversation, and I can clearly remember the moment, as we passed by stunning snow-topped mountains, my new husband asked me, 'If you could have done anything for a career, what would you have done?'

I told him I would have finished the journalism degree that I'd started, with a vision to become editor of *Women's Health* magazine. It was the first time I'd really stared this ambition in the face, and certainly the first time I'd said it out loud. I realised I wanted to have a career learning and communicating, in a vibrant and creative space that allowed me to positively affect people's wellbeing.

What came next was a light-bulb moment, which on reflection was the first step in my own rewiring. (I just didn't know it yet.) I said, 'Actually, I could probably get myself back on that pathway by starting a blog or something'. My awareness was sparked, and this is the first step in self-directed neuroplasticity.

Awareness is the ignition that cues your nervous system to pay attention. Neuroscience tells us that this isn't just 'nice to have' but instead sets up the conditions for rewiring. Studies on self-directed neuroplasticity show that conscious awareness and controlled attention in the prefrontal cortex are what allow you to notice patterns, regulate emotions, and shift behaviour over time. Without this conscious awareness, your brain defaults to autopilot, replaying old predictions and habits.

This is why journalling, coaching conversations or even a probing question from a partner can feel so powerful. They act like a spotlight, shifting you out of unconscious prediction and into conscious awareness. The first step in any experiment is getting honest about what is — not what you wish were true or what social media tells you should be true.

The horizon-setting framework I outline in chapter 3 provides this foundation by broadly generating awareness of what you want and your underlying values and drivers. When you run the Experiment Mindset loop, you then get as specific as you can about what you want to learn, change or achieve. This brings an immense amount of attention to it, creating an environment for neuroplastic change.

Thankfully, both self-awareness and the ability to regulate your attention can also be trained. (See chapter 3 for more in this area.)

Experience

Experience is gained through engaging in an activity that has you interacting with your environment. But when it comes to neuroplastic change, it can't be just any activity. Novelty, unpredictability and even friction are what drive your brain to update itself. This is why scrolling social feeds — which is predictable, curated and safe — doesn't change you. Contrast that with having a tough conversation, lifting a heavier weight than you thought you could or travelling somewhere you've never been before. The resistance or friction is important. Growth isn't meant to feel cushy and easy. It needs to be at least a little bit hard.

As discussed earlier in this chapter, however, this extra work is metabolically expensive — and so the brain resists it. To overcome this resistance, you need to offer a reward. Studies on the anterior mid-cingulate cortex (aMCC) — a part of the brain associated with motivation, the perception–action cycle and tenacity — show we only commit to effortful change when the potential reward outweighs the energetic cost. In other words, if the juice isn't worth the squeeze, your brain will default back to the old pathway. That's why it's so important to design experiments that matter enough to you that the friction feels worth it. Again, the horizon-setting framework in the next chapter helps point you in the right direction, which is why it's a part of the pre-work.

Reflection

Reflection is how you integrate experience. Without it, the lesson doesn't 'stick'. This part mirrors the brain's predictive process—comparing what actually happened with what you thought would happen. This is the point where new pathways are either reinforced or begin to be pruned away.

In practice, reflection can be as simple as asking:

- What did I expect?
- What actually happened?
- What does this tell me about myself or the world?

This is where thinking like a curious scientist really pays off. Instead of berating yourself for 'failing' if the result was something other than what you expected, you treat the result as data. That data is what updates your prediction machine for next time. If your experiment was really successful, the positive reinforcement you experience will encourage the repetition and embedding of the change.

Consolidation (rest)

Sleep, rest and downtime are not luxuries. This is when you have the physical environment that allows new neural connections to strengthen so that growth can happen. Research shows that during sleep the brain prunes unnecessary connections, consolidates memory and clears waste. (See, for example, 'The consequences of sleep deprivation on cognitive performance' by Mohammad Khan and Hamdan Al-Jahdali.) If you skip rest, you mess with the process, which is why chronic stress or sleep deprivation makes change feel impossible.

These steps of awareness, experience, reflection and consolidation create the underlying structure of the Experiment Mindset, and can literally reshape your brain in ways that support emotional regulation, motivation and wellbeing. Far from self-help fluff, this process is based on neuroscience.

Embracing the struggle

As touched on earlier, the success of my coaching clients almost always correlates with their willingness to embrace the struggle. When someone comes to coaching hoping for an easy short cut, they rarely achieve what they set out to. But the ones who decide to embrace the discomfort, awkwardness and fear are the ones who grow.

When it comes to growth, I'll back someone with tenacity over someone with a high IQ any day of the week, and this insight was the reason I decided to research the Experiment Mindset in the first place. I'd already been using experimentation as the mechanism to reduce the barrier to entry of leaning into the tough stuff. Using challenges as an opportunity to gather data was something I'd been doing intuitively, and for a long time I thought the success that came was just a pattern I noticed. Then I discovered the emerging neuroscience that backs it up.

Exercising your growth muscle

As mentioned, the aMCC area in your brain is associated with motivation and resilience, and it helps you weigh up whether the effort of any action is worth the reward. It's the part that kicks in when you're deciding, 'Do I drag myself to the gym after work, or do I head straight for the couch?' Researchers have found that damage to the aMCC leads to apathy and a lack of drive.

Emerging evidence on the flip side to this suggests that this part of the brain is likely trainable. Early studies (for example, from Eliana

Vassena and colleagues) hint that people who repeatedly put themselves in effortful situations, such as athletes and performers, show differences in the size and connectivity of this region compared to those who don't. In those with symptoms of apathy, this region of the brain is smaller. Choosing hard things might literally strengthen the circuits that make it easier to keep choosing hard things. Every time you step up and do something that feels uncomfortable, you may be training yourself to be able to do so more in the future, in any domain. The struggle itself could be rewiring you to better handle the next challenge.

This trait of human potential can't be ignored. You need to embrace the struggle of growth, and even learn to love it.

This is why the Experiment Mindset works so well. It reduces the barrier to entry to trying something difficult. You know you'll either succeed or you'll learn. This increases the likelihood that you'll gather new experiences, complete with the required friction and novelty. Then the process of consolidating that learning through reflection and gathering the data is built in.

Growth is no longer a path to be followed. It's a system to be run, and the system correlates directly with how your brain grows. In the next chapter, we look at how you can make sure you're driving growth that's personal, practical and lasting.

Reflection prompts

- Think about yourself ten years ago. What's different now? What does that tell you about how much change is still possible in the next 10 years?
- Where in your life right now are you stuck in awareness without taking action? What's one small experience you could create this week to start building a new pathway?

3

Testing what works for you with the N-of-1 approach

A few years ago, I read *Finding Ultra* by Rich Roll. He's a pretty famous podcaster and endurance athlete who turned his life around when he was approaching 40 by overcoming addiction and adopting a plant-based lifestyle. I was so inspired by his story that I decided to try the diet myself. My hypothesis was simple: if eating a plant-based diet had given Rich more energy and better long-term health, maybe it could do the same for me.

So I committed—60 days, all in. I downloaded an app, stocked the fridge with tofu and tempeh, and got curious about the results I might get. At the time, I was training at a CrossFit gym and, about two weeks in to my new regime, I noticed something was off. I was dragging myself through sessions, my whole body was feeling heavy and tired, and I had no oomph. I just couldn't find the power or strength I usually had, no matter how hard I tried. But I was sleeping fine, eating what I thought was well and consistently, and training regularly, so short of having some kind of illness, I started to consider that my experiment might be giving me an unexpected result.

I recorded it in my journal, and I told my CrossFit coach (an ex-army guy who was a bit of a hard nut) about my lack of oomph. He just looked at me blankly, as if to say, 'toughen up'. Maybe I did need to toughen up, but something didn't feel right so I got bloodwork done just in case. It turned out my iron levels were so low I had developed iron-deficiency anaemia. Could I have adjusted, learned how to be a better vegan, and made it work? Possibly. But the truth was I didn't love plant-based living enough to stick with it. So I reintroduced meat, took some supplements, and within weeks I felt myself again.

That experiment gave me my answer. I'd formed a hypothesis, applied information, gathered personalised data, gained knowledge about myself and become a little wiser. What worked for Rich Roll didn't work for me, and what works for me might not work for you. But because I treated the experiment as a live test, not a change to my belief system, I didn't lose out. I grew. I was one step closer to knowing the best way for me to eat to optimise my own wellbeing.

General evidence gives you possibilities. Experiments give you answers.

I'd become my own N-of-1.

Understanding why N-of-1 trials can be so powerful

An 'N-of-1' study is one where an experiment is run on a single subject. Instead of looking at averages, a researcher can gather data on a single person to see what holds true just for them. It's the best form of individualisation. Doctors might test different pain medications on the same patient, for example, to see what actually works for them.

The key idea is that evidence doesn't just exist at the population level. It can be built for the individual.

In the context of personal growth, this concept means you can identify what works specifically for you, rather than just throwing stuff at the wall and hoping that it sticks.

N-of-1 case study: The asthma patient and the wrong drug

Back in the 1980s, doctors at McMaster University in Canada worked with an asthma patient who was taking theophylline, a drug considered to be standard treatment for asthma at the time. On paper, the evidence said it should help. But the patient wasn't improving.

So the doctors ran an N-of-1 trial. Over several weeks, the patient alternated between theophylline and a placebo, keeping a daily symptom diary. The data showed every time the patient took the drug, symptoms got worse. When they stopped and instead took the placebo, symptoms improved, even with fewer steroids.

That single trial changed everything for that one person. Instead of being locked into 'best practice' based on averages, they discovered the drug was harming them rather than helping. What looked like evidence-based medicine at the population level was the wrong evidence for their body.

That's the power of N-of-1. It takes the general and makes it personal.

The post-truth era

This individualised testing is even more important today because most of us aren't reading the findings of highly researched randomised control trials or literature reviews. Instead, we're listening to old mate on a viral podcast, a rambling politician with an underlying agenda or our favourite Instagram influencer. And even when 'research' is presented to us, it's getting increasingly difficult to trust what's valid and sound.

If I logged in to my social media right now, I could easily see 'evidence' of the benefits of zone 2 endurance training, heavy strength training, Pilates or yoga, and the dangers of them all, within just a few quick scrolls.

In her book *Prove It*, Australian science journalist Elizabeth Finkel describes the time we're in as the 'post-truth era'. This is a time when the foundations of the scientific method—the process of observing, asking questions, and seeking answers through tests and experiments—becomes more crucial than ever to give us some clarity and direction. We need a real source of rational truth.

The problem with population studies

Most of the advice we're sold is at best built on population studies, and they do have value. They tell us what tends to work on average across large groups of people, and they help shape guidelines, inform best practice and point us toward strategies worth trying. But averages hide variation. What works beautifully for 60 per cent of people may do nothing for you and, in some cases it may even backfire (like with my dabble with veganism).

A 2024 review by John Noone and colleagues (published in *Cell Metabolism*) showed that extrinsic factors such as sleep, diet, stress, circadian rhythms, along with intrinsic factors such as genetics, age, sex and hormonal status, drive enormous variation in how different people respond to the very same stimulus. Two people can follow the same intervention and get completely different outcomes.

This is why general evidence can only ever give you possibilities; your experiments give you answers.

I worked with a woman once who lost huge amounts of weight by following an intermittent fasting diet. The change was incredible, until her hair started falling out. She was so invested in her approach, however, that she wasn't willing to consider that her diet may be causing her hair loss. She'd also created an echo chamber for herself. She'd gone deep into all of the fasting books, and her social media algorithms were geared to show her what she wanted to see—that fasting was the answer, it only provided benefits, and anyone who tried to tell her otherwise was wrong. She had blinders on because she wasn't doing the reflection part of the experiment equation. Instead, she'd doubled-down on her belief.

In a world drowning in content, many of us cling harder to the phrase 'evidence-based'. We want certainty. We want the guarantee that something will work before we even begin. But 'evidence-based' doesn't mean it's automatically right for your biology, your context or your stage of life. Treating yourself like a participant in an N-of-1 experiment isn't about rejecting evidence but personalising it. You take what's been shown to work in general, and you test it in your own life to see if it holds true for you. That's how you move from guessing to knowing, and from information to wisdom.

The failed open-office experiment

For decades, companies were sold on the idea that open offices were the future of work. Architects and executives believed that tearing down walls would spark creativity, collaboration and culture. The logic seemed sound: sociologists had shown that proximity drives interaction, and surveys suggested people liked the idea of fewer barriers. On paper, it looked like progress.

(continued)

So workplaces across Australia (and the world) have repeated the same patterns. Organisations have ripped out partitions and scrapped private offices, and replaced them with vast, open spaces. The change was framed as 'evidence-based', drawing on theories of proximity, survey results about employee satisfaction and the growing architectural trend of transparency. But what it lacked was hard behavioural data. No-one had really measured what happened when you put actual people in these environments day after day.

That's what Harvard researchers Ethan Bernstein and Stephen Turban set out to do in 2018. They tracked two Fortune 500 companies as they shifted thousands of employees into open-plan spaces. Using wearable devices to measure real-time interaction, they captured what people actually did, not what they said they'd do on a survey.

The result was the opposite of what the broad studies had predicted. Face-to-face interaction fell by around 70 per cent. Communication via email and instant message spiked instead of dropping. Employees withdrew, put on headphones, and did whatever they could to carve out privacy. Instead of rising, collaboration collapsed.

The earlier 'evidence' wasn't fabricated. It was just incomplete. Surveys and theories told one story, but lived experience told another. This is why averages and population studies are never the full answer. They can point you in a direction, but until you run the experiment in your own context, you don't know how the results will really play out.

Imagine if these workplaces operated with an Experiment Mindset, setting their own small N-of-1 (or even N-of-5 or N-of-10) experiment in a test zone instead of rearranging their entire buildings?

Before you overhaul your entire approach, the important questions to ask are 'What's the smallest version of this change I could test safely?' and 'What is my minimum viable experiment?'

The antidote for perfectionism

Getting stuck in perfectionism is another trap you can easily fall into. You worry you might fail in a big and public way, like the organisations that went all-in on their workplace re-design, or even in a small way, like I did when I depleted my body by following the wrong eating philosophy for me. Perfectionism thrives on the idea that one 'right' answer is possible—a single path that's the best choice—and that you have to find it before you act. This idea keeps you stuck in endless analysis, waiting until you feel certain, until you feel ready. You're taking action in the background, doing all the prep work to try to get it right. Then you come to your answer, go all-in without gathering personalised data, and it's not right. *Cue shame spiral.*

Scientists don't work this way. While perfectionism may hate uncertainty, scientists love it. They know that what doesn't work is just as valuable as what does, because the findings add clarity about the future. They know that growth isn't linear, and failure isn't final. Each experiment is simply a data-gathering exercise.

Scientists don't just gather more information. They gather data.

Taking advantage of the Feedback/Action Matrix

The sweet spot on your growth plan depends on your balance between action and feedback. In short, if you're waiting to be ready, you're starting too late. Start, suck, gather your lessons, figure it out and then get good. This is the only way to grow. The following figure highlights how you can plot feedback against action, and how this influences the mindset you're breeding.

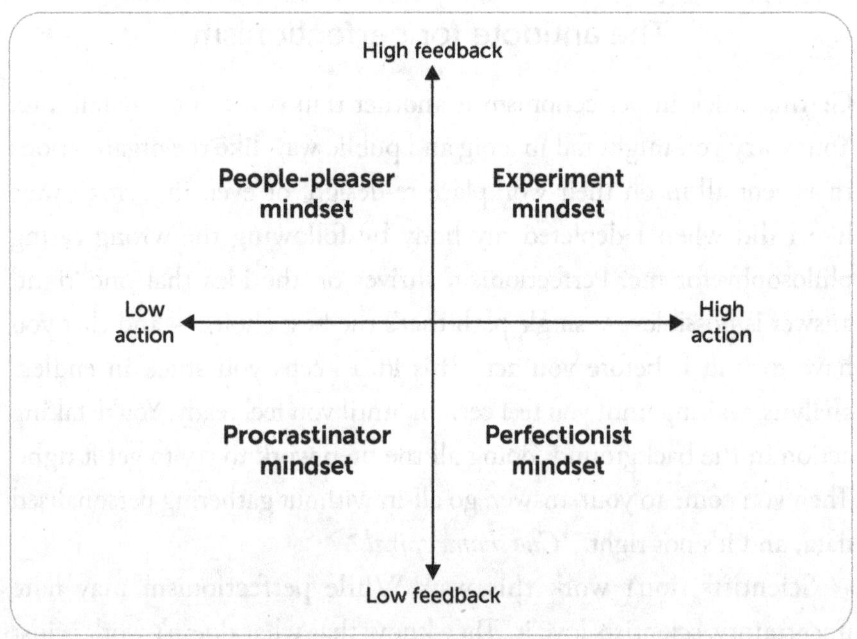

Mindsets across the Feedback/Action Matrix

Low action/high feedback

If you're more focused on the feedback you're receiving than taking action, you're a people pleaser, gathering input from everyone around you to make sure it's okay before you move. That's a nice way to grow into someone else's plan for you.

Low action/low feedback

Procrastination lives in the low action/low feedback quadrant of the Feedback/
Action Matrix, normally bred by fear, uncertainty, overwhelm and boredom,
or a capability gap. Both taking action and seeking feedback can help shift
you. If you really don't know how to do what you need to do, ask someone
who has done it before you. If you do know but you're scared, what's the
minimal viable action you can take to begin gathering data and momentum?

High action/low feedback

If you gravitate towards the high action/low feedback quadrant, hello
familiar friend, you're a perfectionist. You're working your butt off to
get it right, before putting it out into the world. Perfectionists tend to
focus on achieving perfect results, looking to the end game rather than
the process. If this is your approach, you're missing out on gathering
valuable feedback, and so not learning and growing in the process. And
even if you achieve your goal, you tend to feel unsatisfied. If you're
anything like me, someone saying, 'You've done a fine job' hits the
same as not reaching the goal at all. Your aim is excellence, or it's
nothing. And while it feels noble to strive for excellence, you're actually
stunting your growth. Likely, you'll find yourself swinging between this
quadrant and low action/low feedback quadrant of the procrastinator.
If you can't get it right the first time, you might delay even starting.

If this is you, you're not alone — indeed, perfectionism is on the rise.
A study by Thomas Curran from the London School of Economics (and
author of *The Perfection Trap*) found that perfectionism is increasing
rapidly, up around 40 per cent since 1989 and particularly among more
recent generations. That's concerning because it's associated strongly
with poor mental health outcomes such as depression and anxiety. It's
something you need to be paying attention to, and something that the
Experiment Mindset can help you to overcome.

High feedback/high action

When the goal becomes learning and data gathering, rather than achieving a perfect outcome, perfectionism becomes unnecessary. Your focus moves to the process, not the end game. Beware, though, that a common trap can be confusing 'learning through *information* gathering' with 'learning through *data* gathering'. Simply gathering more information is procrastination in disguise.

Working out what you are experimenting toward

The Feedback/Action Matrix highlights the need to balance action and feedback. And, as already emphasised, the Experiment Mindset is all about starting before you're ready and gathering data as you go, understanding that what works for someone else might not work for you. But the questions that might be on your mind, because they stump most of us, are, *What do I even want?* and *What am I testing toward?*

You can run all the experiments you want, and gather all the data in the world, but if you don't know what you're actually trying to learn about yourself, you're just wandering.

You need direction. You don't need a rigid plan or a five-year roadmap that will be outdated in six months, but you do need enough clarity to know whether an experiment is moving you closer to who you want to become, or further away from this. This is where the Horizon Builder comes in.

Introducing the Horizon Builder

When I work with my coaching clients, I don't ask them about their five-year plan or their career goals. I want them to dig for something different. I ask the question that most people struggle with: *What do you want?*

Faced with this, most people look at me like I've asked them to solve a physics equation in another language. Like too many of us, they've been so focused on the next destination, the title, the salary, the house, the achievement, that they've forgotten, or perhaps avoided, thinking about what they actually want for themselves.

When you articulate what you want, your brain shifts its attentional filters. Clarity changes what becomes visible. The right future pulls you toward it. That's why I created the Horizon Builder.

Rather than a rigid five-year plan that will be obsolete before the ink dries, my Horizon Builder provides a compass that helps you set your direction without having to know every step along your path. You have enough clarity to make decisions, along with enough flexibility to adapt when life throws you a curveball (which it inevitably will).

The Horizon Builder asks questions in six specific areas:

1. *Place:* Where do you want to be? Think 'setting' more than 'address' — not, 'I want to live in Sydney' and more like, 'I want to live somewhere I can walk to work', 'I want to be near the ocean', 'I want to be in a city where things are happening' or 'I want to be surrounded with loads of windows and a room full of plants'.
2. *People:* Who do you want to be surrounded with? Consider the type of people who give you energy or inspire you. Your answer might be, 'I want to be around energised people who challenge me', 'I want to be around people who are building things' or 'I want colleagues who don't take themselves too seriously'.
3. *State:* How do you want to feel on an ordinary Tuesday? Calm? Energised? Present? We often think a lot about how we want to feel on holidays or when we're crushing a goal, but rarely think

about how we want to feel on a random, unremarkable Tuesday afternoon. These 'boring' bits, rather than the inflection points, make up most of your life, and they're the moments you should be thinking about.

4. *Skills:* What capabilities (intellectual, emotional, creative or physical) do you want to develop? What do you want to be able to do that you can't do now? What do you want to get better at? What do you want to learn? Humans need a sense of mastery to stay inspired enough to grow.

5. *Values:* What principles will you refuse to trade, even under pressure? These are your non-negotiables — the things you stand for and the lines you won't cross. You'll defend these principles even when it's uncomfortable.

6. *Impact:* What mark do you want to make? This is your meaning and the difference you want to make in the world, and it can be as big or small as you like. Yours could be, 'I want to help people feel less alone', 'I want to build something that lasts' or 'I want to solve a problem that matters'.

Instead of chaining yourself to rigid outcomes, the Horizon Builder makes it safe for you to be what I call 'rebelliously vague'. You're building in room for flexibility while still giving yourself enough direction to guide decisions. You don't have to know the exact job title, the postcode or the LinkedIn headline. You just need a true north.

When you have your horizon set, every experiment you run has a clear purpose. You're not just trying random things to see what sticks. You're testing whether this action, this choice, this change moves you closer to the person you want to become.

That's how the N-of-1 approach becomes powerful. You're gathering personalised data, but you're gathering it with intention.

Setting your horizon

Have a go at setting your horizon for yourself. Allow yourself to let your barriers fall away. Don't worry about what's practical or possible for now, we'll focus on that in later chapters. For now, just let yourself dream.

Answer the overall *'What do you want?'* question by working out your responses in the following six areas:

- *Places:* Where do you want to be? (Think 'setting' more than 'address'.)
- *People:* Who do you want to be surrounded with? (Consider the type of people who give you energy or inspire you.)
- *State:* How do you want to feel on an ordinary Tuesday? (Calm? Energised? Present?)
- *Skills:* What capabilities (intellectual, emotional, creative or physical) do you want to develop?
- *Values:* What principles will you refuse to trade, even under pressure?
- *Impact:* What mark do you want to make?

Remember Emma from chapter 1? Setting her eyes on her horizon was where the shift really started for her. She stopped thinking in titles and started opening up to a broader life vision—one that, for just a moment, let her list of barriers fall away.

Her body knew before her brain did. Her shoulders dropped. She exhaled. Considering the horizon she had just envisioned, she said, 'That sounds...possible, actually'. She followed this immediately with, 'But I don't know where to start'.

That's when the real work began.

From information to wisdom

As you set your eyes on your horizon, becoming your own N-of-1 helps you find a pathway that works specifically for you.

We have more access to knowledge than any generation in history—including through podcasts, books, courses and articles. We should be the smartest, fittest, most productive and most fulfilled humans to ever walk the earth. And we're not. A gap exists between what we know and what we do. Bridging this gap comes through what you do with the information you collect.

At its simplest, you can think of it like this:

- Data is your raw observations about your life.
- Information is what you learn from other people's research, experience or content.
- Action is when you apply that information to your own data.
- Reflection gives you the opportunity to learn what happens specifically for you, and what to do with that information.
- Wisdom is what you build when you repeat that cycle over time.

In other words, information becomes powerful when you combine it with action and reflection. That's when it stops being 'interesting' and starts becoming personally true.

In chapter 8, I explore this idea, and what I call the Wisdom Cycle, in much more detail. I also outline exactly how to use this cycle to turn your experiments into personalised insight. For now, all you need to remember is this:

- Information doesn't build wisdom; experience does.
- General evidence provides possibilities.
- Your experiments give you answers.
- You are the subject.

- You are the research.
- You are the data.

In the next part, we're going to take a look at where to start with your experiments.

Reflection prompts

◆ Where in your life are you stuck at the 'information' stage—consuming content but not gathering your own data? (This might include podcasts, books or courses you've consumed but haven't applied.)

◆ What's one area where you've been avoiding looking at the data because it's uncomfortable? What data is your body, your finances, your relationships or your team's performance providing? What would you see if you actually measured this data?

◆ What's one experiment you could run this week to nudge you in even a tiny way toward your horizon?

The foundations of experimental living

Your brain is always guessing what might happen next. Most of the time, it guesses right, so you cruise on autopilot. But when reality doesn't match the prediction—when you try something new, feel friction or experience surprise—when your brain pays attention. And that's when change becomes possible.

The problem is we spend most of our lives trying to avoid that friction, sticking to what's familiar, what's worked before and what feels safe. This approach is practical and seems efficient, but efficiency and growth don't always go hand in hand.

In this part of the book, you've seen that:

- *Growth requires specific conditions:* Your brain can change, but only when you create the right environment for neuroplastic change: awareness, focused experience, reflection and rest. Reading about growth isn't the same as growing. Thinking about change isn't the same as changing.
- *What works for someone else might not work for you:* Rich Roll's plant-based transformation made him an ultra-endurance athlete. It made me anaemic. General evidence gives you possibilities, but your experiments give you answers. You need to become your own N-of-1.
- *Direction matters more than rigid plans:* The Horizon Builder gives you a compass, not a map. You don't need to know every step, you just need to know what you're testing toward: the places, people, state, skills, values and impact that matter to you.

You've also learned that:

- progress and growth aren't the same thing
- straight lines are a myth in a non-linear world

- your brain updates itself through prediction errors, not perfect execution
- the struggle isn't a bug in the system—it's how the system works
- data becomes knowledge, knowledge becomes information, and information becomes wisdom through repeated cycles of action and reflection.

You now understand *why* people stay stuck and *how* your brain actually changes, and that growth must be individualised. But knowing you need personalised experiments doesn't tell you what to experiment with. That's where the three levers come in. In part II, I outline exactly what you can pull when you're ready to run your first experiment.

Reflection prompts

- When you think about your horizon—the person you want to become—what's the biggest gap between who you are now and who you'd need to be to get there?
- What would change if you treated your next decision as an experiment rather than a commitment?

PART II
The three levers for growth

In the chapters in the previous part, I outlined how growth works and explained the science behind it. However, something that most books on personal growth miss is that growth doesn't happen in a vacuum. It happens in the context of your real life—inside a whole ecosystem of influencing factors that are either helping you grow or capping your potential.

Your growth is shaped by the following three underlying levers that are working on you all the time, whether you're aware of them or not:

1. *Environment:* The people, places and prompts around you.
2. *Physiology:* Your brain and body's capacity.
3. *Psychology:* Your beliefs, mindset and identity.

As shown in the following figure, these levers are interconnected and overlapping.

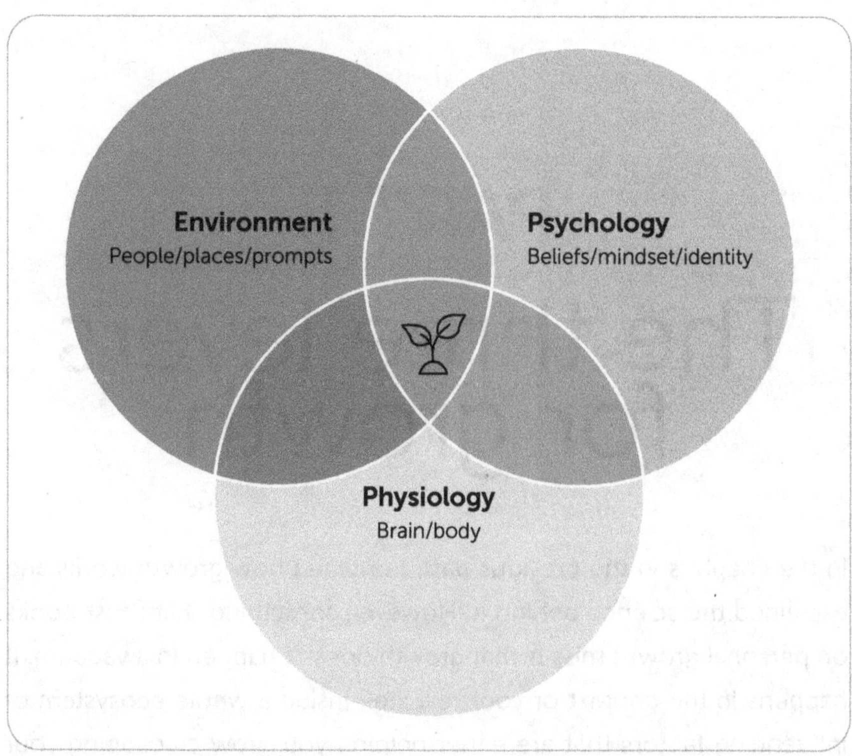

The three levers for growth

If your environment makes the old behaviour easier than the new one, your physiology is depleted and you're operating in 'low power mode', or if your psychology is holding onto an old identity that doesn't fit anymore, your experiment won't stick. It doesn't matter how perfectly executed it is.

Most people focus on changing behaviour because that's what's obvious, but behaviour is rarely the problem. Instead, it's a symptom. The problem is you're pulling on the wrong lever.

This part shows you how to identify which lever is stopping you, and how to pull the one that actually matters.

Ready? Let's start with your environment.

4

Environment

Carl Rogers was a pioneer of humanistic psychology, an approach that focuses on human potential and personal growth. It's the same approach that famous psychologist Abraham Maslow was also a pioneer of, and one I align with closely. It's grounded in the belief that every person has the capacity for self-actualisation, and that when the right conditions exist, we naturally move toward becoming more of who we are.

Rogers grew up on a farm, and he often shared a story about finding a box of potatoes in his family's cold, dark basement. The only light in that basement came from a small window near the ceiling. Even with almost no sunlight, no warmth and nothing that should have supported life, each potato had sent out long, thin shoots reaching for that crack of light. The shoots were pale and fragile, rather than the thick green ones produced by potatoes planted in healthy soil, but they were still growing.

He said this reminded him that even under the worst conditions, living things will still reach for the light. Deep within us is a force that wants to become. He called this drive to grow into what we're meant to be 'the actualising tendency' — similar to a flower turning toward the sun.

That image has stayed with me, because it's nice to know we can grow in almost any environment. The adaptability of the human system means you'll bend, stretch and contort yourself into shapes that keep you surviving. But survival growth takes something from you, pulling from the same reserves you need for joy, creativity, fulfilment and connection. These are your green, rich shoots, or your life force. The longer you stay in survival growth, the harder it becomes to remember what real growth feels like.

Thriving isn't about being stronger than your environment, but about shaping an environment that helps you grow. That's what Rogers meant when he talked about turning towards the sun, and what neuroscience confirms. Your brain is constantly scanning for and responding to the signals around you. It'll pick up on the tone of a conversation, the lighting in a room, the people you spend time with, and the physical places and things that are easiest for you to get to. Those cues in your environment tell it what to do next.

When you start designing those cues intentionally, you stop fighting for light and start turning toward it.

In this chapter, I outline how to work with the following three layers of your environment that shape who you become:

1. *People:* Who you surround yourself with.
2. *Places:* Where you spend your time.
3. *Prompts:* The small cues that signal your brain to act.

You can grow in the dark. Most of us have. But, at some point, the work becomes choosing where you want to grow next and learning how to turn toward the sun.

Considering the people around you

I recently sat down for coffee with James Begley, a client of mine. He's an ex-AFL footballer and now entrepreneur who founded Launchd, a company that uses technology to support brand partnerships. When I arrived, he was just wrapping up a phone call and I caught the end of the conversation. He said something to the person on the other end along the lines of, 'Will it be you taking care of the PR and announcements, or do you want us to do that?' I know it's rude to eavesdrop, but I was pretty intrigued. When he put down the phone I casually acknowledged his wheeling and dealing, and he let me know that he and a group of his friends have just purchased Adelaide Lightning, a women's National Basketball League team.

This triggered a conversation about James's growth. When we met he was founder and CEO of a rapidly expanding business and, respectfully, a bit of a frustrated bottleneck in his business because he was playing outside of his zone of genius and wearing all of the hats. Now? I could see he'd found his sweet spot as an influential creator, building partnerships and inspiring people to come along for the ride.

James has used commitment, increased self-awareness and an Experiment Mindset to get himself into a much better position, both personally and in business. But the power of his networks in bringing in opportunities can't be ignored. Even as we drank our coffee at a restaurant in one of Adelaide's most prestigious suburbs, a man walked over to shake James's hand like an old friend. It turned out he owned the restaurant we were in and also happened to be an investor in James's company. James was honest about the power and privilege that came with his network, a web of sporting connections and private-school links that opened doors most people never see. You can debate the fairness of it, but the truth is it exists. You can strategically build and leverage the power of the people you surround yourself with, or not. You might not have the leg-up that James had through his AFL career, but you do have the power to change. And this runs deeper than people within social networks simply supporting each other.

Working out if your network equals your net worth

You've no doubt heard Jim Rohn's famous claim that each of us is a product of the five people we spend the most time with. It's a claim repeated in leadership programs, podcasts and personal growth workshops like a law of physics. The idea is to choose your five people wisely, and surround yourself with people who are already where you want to be. It's catchy, but it's not quite true—not in the way you think, anyway.

You are influenced by the people closest to you, but the influence doesn't stop there. It extends much further than that.

Researchers Nicholas Christakis and James Fowler discovered this when they studied decades of data from one of the largest and longest-running health studies ever conducted, the Framingham Heart Study. Extraordinarily, what they found was that our behaviour, emotions and even physical health are shaped not just by our friends, but also by our friends' friends, and even their friends.

In what they termed 'social contagion theory', if a friend of yours becomes obese, you're 45 per cent more likely to gain weight yourself within a few years. If a friend of that friend gains weight, your risk still rises by 20 per cent. Even someone three degrees removed, a friend of a friend of a friend, has a measurable influence on your body, habits and sense of what's normal. The same is true for smoking, happiness, generosity and political views. And it doesn't take much to see this idea stretching into business and career success.

Your life is being shaped not by five people but by hundreds, creating an invisible web of influence that extends well beyond your awareness. The reason isn't magic but norms. When enough people in your social network behave in a certain way, your brain recalibrates what's acceptable, safe and possible. In this recalibration, your baseline shifts.

You want to spend time in groups where your desired behaviour is the normal behaviour. That's how social contagion works. You absorb not just behaviour but also expectation.

Taking advantage of the Pygmalion effect

Another way people can influence your environment and expectations is through what's known as the 'Pygmalion effect' — the finding that we each tend to rise or fall to meet the expectations placed on us. When someone believes you're capable, your brain reads that as safety and potential, rather than threat. You stretch a little further. You try again. When someone expects less, you unconsciously shrink to fit that frame. Your sense of possibility expands or contracts based on the social cues around you.

This is another reason the people in your life matter so much — not just for who they are, but also for what they mirror back to you. You're influenced by their behaviour, while also being shaped by their belief in who you can become.

Setting your bar high

When you surround yourself with people who see your potential, your brain receives a continuous stream of signals that growth is possible and safe. When you spend time in relationships where you have to earn belonging, or where the bar is set low, you'll behave accordingly.

The following figure highlights how the Pygmalion effect becomes a cycle of reinforced behaviour and expectations.

(continued)

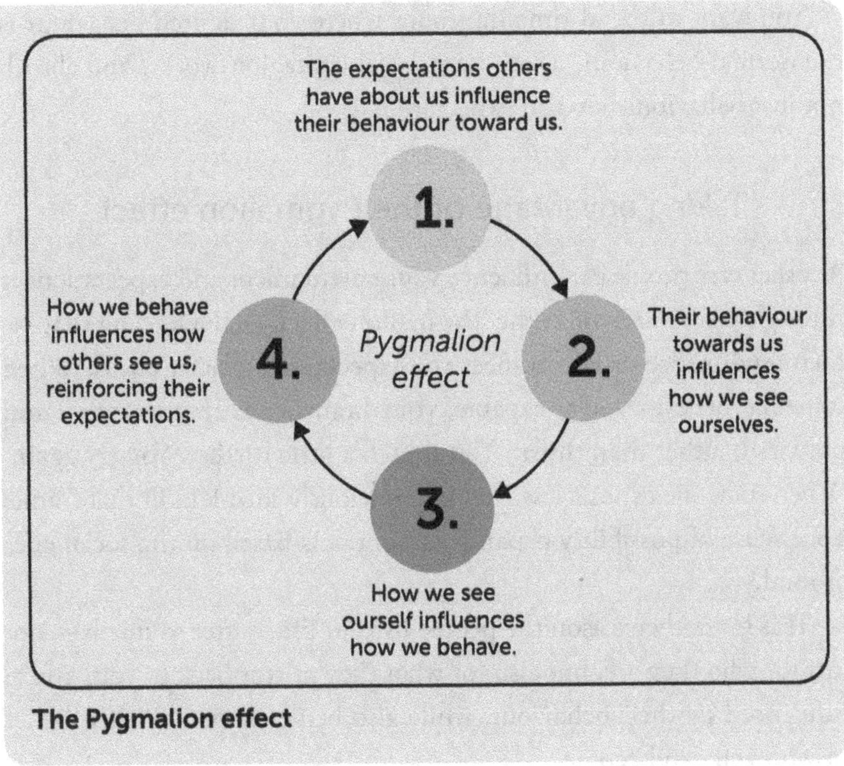

The Pygmalion effect

The work, then, isn't just about choosing 'better' people. It's about becoming conscious of the emotional and behavioural signals your relationships send to your brain. The people around you are part of your environment, and part of the cues your brain uses to decide whether to turn toward the sun or stay curled underground.

Over time, I've come to see that most relationships fall into three relationship archetypes:

- *Expanders:* These people act as sunlight. They help you stretch your sense of what's possible and lift your game. These are usually people who are ahead of you on the path you want to travel along, or people who are doing great and interesting things in the world. They'll stretch but not judge you, because they know what it's like to embrace the struggle of growth.

- *Sustainers:* These people are like soil. They steady and support you when things get hard, and bring you back down to earth when you need it. These are usually peers, great friends or family.
- *Drainers:* These people shade your sunshine. They drain you, often without meaning to, and pull you back into old patterns or ways of thinking that limit growth. It's nice to think you can avoid drainers, but it's not always possible. Sometimes they might be family or friends who mean well and want to keep you safe. The key is to be aware of this tendency, and balance their input with your expanders and sustainers, as well as your vision for yourself.

All three have a place in your life, but growth depends on recognising which is which, and designing your environment accordingly.

Micro-experiment: People audit

Growth doesn't happen in isolation. It happens in context, and your context is full of people. You don't need to burn your whole network down or curate some perfect inner circle. You just need to get clear on where your energy and possibility are coming from and where they're being drained.

This is a simple experiment to help you do that.

Step 1: Map your network

Create a table similar to the one provided to list your:

- *Expanders:* The people who stretch your thinking, model what's possible and make you want to raise your game in your targeted growth area.

(continued)

◆ *Sustainers:* The people who hold you steady, remind you who you are, and bring calm or clarity when you need it.

◆ *Drainers:* The people or dynamics that pull you back into old patterns, even when they don't mean to.

Be honest, but don't overthink it. This isn't about judging people—it's about observing data.

Expanders	Sustainers	Drainers

Step 2: Look for imbalance

What do you notice? Are you surrounded by too many sustainers and not enough expanders? Do you keep drainers close out of obligation or habit? Or have you built a circle so aspirational that you rarely feel grounded?

Your brain calibrates its baseline for 'normal' from the people you spend time with. If everyone around you is unmotivated or cynical, you'll adapt to survive there. If curiosity, courage and play are the norm, you'll adapt to that instead.

Step 3: Adjust the mix

If you have noticed an imbalance in the people around you, run an experiment to adjust the mix. Start with your hypothesis and then work through the method to gather your data.

Hypothesis: Changing one relationship pattern, even slightly, will shift my energy, focus or motivation.

Method:

1. Choose one small adjustment to test this week:
   ◆ Spend one intentional hour with an expander who inspires you.

- ◆ Reconnect with a sustainer who steadies you.
- ◆ Create subtle distance (via a pause, a no or a boundary) with one drainer.

2. Observe what happens over the next seven days:

- ◆ How does your energy change?
- ◆ What emotions or ideas surface more easily?
- ◆ Do you notice a difference in your motivation or creativity?

3. Record your data.

Step 4: Reflect:

What did this experiment tell you about the kind of relational environment that helps you grow? Is it time to make that small shift permanent, or test another?

Remember: You don't have to overhaul your whole network. You just have to notice how it shapes you, and start turning a little more toward the light.

Focusing on places and prompts

Your growth is shaped by not just *who* you surround yourself with but also *what* you surround yourself with. Environment, context and culture can either accelerate or inhibit who you become — and one of Australia's most extreme and perhaps most controversial experiments on the power of environment is happening right now inside the prison system.

The Macquarie Correctional Centre, built in central New South Wales in 2018, is a high-security facility that houses inmates convicted of serious crimes, including murder, rape and terrorism. But unlike traditional prisons, Macquarie operates on a radically different philosophy.

Here, inmates work long, structured days, up to 15 hours, in trades such as design and welding. They live in dormitory-style pods rather than cells. They have access to art classes, gymnasiums, music lessons and even a prison cafe that serves milkshakes. In 2025, an inmate was awarded a PhD for prison garden design. This is a far cry from the typical image of incarceration, where prisoners are locked down and fed barely edible meals. For some, this might feel uncomfortably soft, and perhaps not what they think 'justice' should look like for our worst offenders. And yet, the early data is worth paying attention to.

In Australia's *Breaking Badness* podcast, former homicide detective Gary Jubelin goes inside Macquarie, interviews its inmates and explores this new model of rehabilitation. At the time of writing, around 13 000 people are in New South Wales prisons, a number that's risen by about 2500 over the past decade. Half of those released will reoffend and return to prison within two years. Macquarie was built partly to address that cycle but, more importantly, to also test whether a change in *context* could change *behaviour*.

The core philosophy is simple: rather than earning privileges through good behaviour, prisoners are given trust, respect and responsibility from day one. If they break that trust, they're transferred to another facility.

In his podcast, Gary describes a tangible shift in the atmosphere of this prison compared to others he's visited. The inmates stand taller. They take pride in their appearance. Their shared spaces are clean and orderly. The constant air of fear and tension that usually fills a prison simply isn't there. Violence is far lower than in a traditional prison. In the five years leading up to the podcast, only two assaults on staff have been recorded—one where an inmate threw a pair of earbuds, and another involving a squirt of water on an officer's back.

Mirroring the Pygmalion effect, the behavioural bar has been set higher, and the prisoners appear to be rising to meet it.

You might feel conflicted about this story, and that's okay. It's not my role in this book to decide whether this model is 'fair'. But it's worth reflecting on what kind of outcome we really want. Because most of these men will eventually walk free to live in communities again. When that day comes, who would you rather as your neighbour? Someone who's been treated like an animal, or someone who's been treated like a human being and given the environment to become one?

The approach is modelled on the Scandinavian prison system, which has the world's lowest re-offending rates. A long-term university study is now underway to track rates of reoffending for those who've served time inside Macquarie, with early signs suggesting the experiment may be working.

Designing environments geared for growth

The Macquarie experiment is a striking example of what behavioural and brain science shows us — that your environment significantly influences your behaviour and can even shape your brain. The same principle applied to the prison environment can also be applied on a smaller scale, to your office, your home, your community and even your phone screen. Every environment is either pulling you toward the person you're becoming or anchoring you to the person you've been.

You don't need to build a new house to redesign your environment. You just need to start noticing the cues that surround you every day and ask a simple question: is this environment training me toward or away from the person I want to be?

The following sections run through the layers of your environment, and their impact on you.

Physical space

Every space you move into influences the way you feel and behave in some way, and this influence can be different for everyone. That's why being your own N-of-1 is so important. Consider the following about the physical space of your environment:

- Clutter and unfinished tasks may cue avoidance and stress. For some, they trigger creativity.
- Natural light, movement and visual order may cue focus and creativity, or relaxation and daydreaming.
- Objects in sight act as prompts for action—for example, a yoga mat, a notebook, a glass of water, cold wine in the fridge or a television on the wall.

The goal isn't aesthetic perfection but functional alignment. Every item in view should remind you of who you're becoming, not who you've been.

Digital space

Your online environment is set up by algorithms as an echo chamber that reinforces your behaviours and beliefs, not as an environment geared for growth—unless you're deliberate about it.

Design your digital space in the same way you'd design your living room—with intention. Remove what drains you, and keep what inspires, stretches and informs you.

Sensory prompts

Sensory prompts are the micro-environmental cues that steer your behaviour. They include the smell of coffee before work, the alarm sound that starts your day and the sticky note that reminds you what to focus your attention on. Small sensory anchors can retrain your system faster than big, complex strategies ever will. They whisper to your brain, 'This is who we are now'.

Micro-experiment: Places and prompts audit

Hypothesis: Changing one cue in my environment will change how easily I can focus, recover or create.

Method:

1. Observe:
   - Spend a day noticing what surrounds you, including your physical, digital and sensory spaces and prompts.
   - Where does your attention go? What happens to your energy? Are you more productive and energised inside or outside? Does the city spark your enthusiasm or creativity? Or are vast open spaces better?
2. Audit:
   - Your categories can remain the same as those used for your people audit, but this time consider the places you spend your time and the environmental prompts around you, and whether these are expanders, sustainers or drainers. Complete a table similar to the one provided. Again, don't overthink it. Trust your first impressions.

Expanders (energise you)	Sustainers (ground you)	Drainers (distract or exhaust)

3. Adjust as needed:
   - Remove or reduce one drain.
   - Add or amplify one expander.
   - Introduce one prompt that cues your desired identity (such as a reminder, object or sound).

(continued)

4. Reflect on the data:

    ◆ Over the next week, notice what shifts in your energy, focus, creativity and calm. Record your data.

Reflection: What surprised you most about how your environment shaped your state? What small change had the biggest return?

Growth happens in context

When you start to notice the subtle cues around you coming from the people, places and prompts in your environment, you realise how much they've been shaping you all along. Your environment is giving your brain instructions about what's safe, what's possible, who you are and who you can be. You don't have to fight those conditions; instead, you can deliberately design them.

The trick is to first become aware of your context and the influence it has on you. The next step is to shape your environment in alignment with who you're becoming, not who you've been. When you do so, growth stops feeling like an uphill battle and becomes something you're supported toward.

But your environment is only part of the story. The second lever for growth is your physiology—your body and brain—because even in the best environment, you can't grow if your system isn't ready. In the next chapter, I outline the physical conditions you need for growth to take root.

Reflection prompts

Consider the following when thinking about the people in your life:

◆ Who in your life stretches your thinking about what's possible right now? When was the last time you spent intentional time with them?

◆ Think about the last week. Who drained your energy? What made that interaction costly, and was it necessary?

◆ If you mapped your current network as expanders, sustainers, and drainers, which category is overrepresented? What does that tell you about why you might feel stuck, steady or growing right now?

Now use the following to think about your environment:

◆ Look around the room you spend your most time in. What does this space tell you about who you're becoming versus who you've been?

◆ What's the first thing you see when you wake up? And what's the last thing you see before bed? Are those cues pulling you toward or away from who you want to be?

◆ Where do you do your best thinking? When did you last give yourself permission to be there?

5

Physiology

I don't know many people who wouldn't describe 2020 as a tough year. The pandemic created incredible uncertainty, stress and hardship globally. I know I'm not alone when I say that on top of the pandemic came a pile on of other stressors, making it one of the toughest years of my life.

From 2016 to 2019, I had worked hard building my consultancy alongside my corporate role and I was rising quickly. I was working with dream clients in an exciting business partnership. I also had a new role at work utilising the new skills I had been building, and life had changed dramatically from the days of not knowing whether I was capable of enjoying my work or not. I was loving it. By now, I had two little boys, the youngest only two, and they were gorgeous, happy and healthy.

As COVID-19 hit, however, people stopped investing in external consultants and leadership development. The organisation I was working for was standing people down without pay, and nothing about my newly formed role was certain.

My dad's health was also spiralling, and he was in and out of hospital. I can remember spending all night in the ICU and having to front up to work calls the next day like nothing had happened. My brother, usually alongside me sharing the load, was living and working overseas, unable to return home as our borders closed.

My nanna, my dad's mum, a very close and important influence in my life, picked up a terrible illness in her nursing home back in my home town and she was in her final months. Eventually, she passed away in September 2020.

On top of that my business partnership ended, causing a couple of years of work and focus to feel wasted, and a close friendship to drift apart.

I had no energy for exercise, and I was managing my anxiety and exhaustion at the end of the day with a glass of wine. Nutrition was whatever I could stomach, and I was living that close to the edge of collapse that a single stressful phone call would cause me to shut down.

Growth was the last thing on my mind; indeed, it felt impossible. So I retreated.

When growth feels impossible

Your brain's most important job isn't to help you grow or fulfil your potential. It would be lovely if that were true, but it isn't. Your brain's most important job is to keep you alive, keep you regulated and meet the needs of your body in any given moment. In her book *How Emotions are Made*, neuroscientist Lisa Feldman Barrett describes this as your 'body budget'. Your brain is constantly allocating resources, energy and attention to keep your body in a working, balanced state, and your personal growth is something it'll only give energy to if the budget has room for it.

I find it helpful to think of this body budget as being similar to the battery on your mobile phone. When my phone is fully charged, my apps run smoothly, I can make calls, write, create, switch between tasks and add more data, and my phone barely skips a beat. But when that battery drops to 20 per cent, a notification pops up offering me the opportunity to switch into low power mode. When the battery on my screen turns to yellow or red rather than green, my phone protects its remaining energy like a precious resource. Functionality becomes limited, background activity shuts down, performance slows and some features simply aren't available.

Your body does the same thing. When you're tired, sick, stressed, under-fuelled, hormonally out of whack or burnt out, your system switches into a kind of biological low power mode. When that happens, the 'nice to haves' such as learning, growth, emotional regulation, creative thinking and resilience, aren't as readily available to you. They're limited because your body is trying to keep you alive, safe and well with the energy it has. It's budgeting.

As mentioned in chapter 2, the three most energy-expensive things you can do are move your body, learn something new and navigate uncertainty. So if your system is already stretched thin, your brain isn't going to prioritise these things. It's going to avoid and limit them.

With this in mind, while your environment creates the context for your growth (as covered in the previous chapter), your physiology is the engine that makes growth possible at all. Every experiment you run, every struggle you come up against, and every change you want to make or habit you want to break relies on the biological energy and neural flexibility available to you in that moment.

When your system is overloaded through things such as not enough sleep, constant stress, chronic illness, poor nutrition or too little movement, change doesn't just *feel* harder. It *is* harder.

That's why when you're exhausted, burnt out or running on adrenaline, you don't grow. You repeat.

I don't want you to get to this point in this chapter and think because you're tired, you have a lot going on in your life, you're stressed out or you're suffering with a chronic illness, you're doomed and you can't grow or evolve in life. Unless you're in the most extreme of circumstances, growth is still possible. However, what is important is gaining awareness of your body budget, understanding where your energy is going and where you have control, and, ideally, finding some ways to add a little more energy to the bank.

Before I talk about using nutrition, sleep and movement to build energy, I need to acknowledge one more physiological force, because it's the one my audiences are talking about the most: stress. It's the thing most likely to drain your body budget, distort your perception of your capacity and interrupt your growth experiments. But, when understood properly, stress can also support them.

The stress paradox

While stress can feel like the ultimate energy drain, it can actually serve as a powerful catalyst for personal growth. Not all stress is bad, and growth is possible if you're stressed. While most of us associate stress with negative outcomes such as burnout, anxiety or overwhelm, it can also be an adaptive force that shapes our potential for growth. Psychologists now call this the 'stress paradox', and you just need to be able to distinguish which type of stress you're experiencing so that you know what to do with it.

Productive stress

Biologically, humans have evolved with a stress response for a reason. It triggers you to take notice of a problem that needs attention, and it motivates you to respond, take action and adapt.

Dr Sharon Bergquist is an internal medicine and lifestyle medicine physician and longevity researcher. In her book *The Stress Paradox: Why You Need Stress to Live Longer, Healthier and Happier*, she argues that mild, intermittent stressors—for example, running experiments that stretch you—are essential for activating the body's repair and adaptation systems. Dr Bergquist prescribes 'microdosing discomfort'—that is, encouraging small, consistent exposures to discomfort to build physiological and psychological resilience. This short, focused and productive stress temporarily sharpens the brain. It increases focus and motivation, along with the neural activity that helps you encode new information.

This kind of stress adds to your energy body budget and supports your growth rather than inhibiting it. However, the next two types of stress don't.

Hypostress

Although discussed more rarely, the first of these negative types of stress is actually relatively common. This stress is 'hypostress', or the stress of understimulation and a lack of challenge. Yes, boredom can stress you out. A study led by Jie Li and published in *BMC Public Health* in 2020 suggests that feeling bored at work is associated with lower life satisfaction, decreased motivation and positive functioning, and increased levels of anxiety and depression.

Stressed by lack of stimulation

Hypostress still drains your body budget, but in a different way. Your system needs a certain level of stimulation, challenge and engagement to stay regulated. When that stimulation drops too low, your brain doesn't relax; it becomes restless. Further evidence of the effect of hypostress was provided by a literature review on boredom and understimulation conducted by Quentin Raffaelli

(continued)

and colleagues, which showed that when your brain can't engage meaningfully with what's in front of you, it starts searching for something else to latch onto. That search burns energy. You become more distractible, less able to focus, more irritable and more prone to rumination. This stress isn't the productive kind that sharpens your attention and growth potential. It's the flat, agitated kind that comes from having nothing that feels purposeful to direct your energy toward.

You don't just get stressed from being busy. You can get stressed from being not busy enough, or being the wrong kind of busy.

Later in this chapter, I provide an exercise that can help you to distinguish how much of your perceived stress lives in this space. Are you feeling stress from challenge? Or stress from tasks that are draining the life out of you?

Hyperstress

Then there's the stress I was experiencing back in 2020: hyperstress. This is a sense of overwhelming pressure, and a feeling that you're being stretched so thin that the demands of your life have overtaken your ability to cope. Many of the leaders I work with live here, juggling competing priorities, never feeling like they're getting on top of things, looking calm on the surface but drowning inside. This kind of stress drains your body battery, steals your focus and gets in the way of your growth.

When stress is chronic or unmanageable like this, it can not only contribute to long-term chronic health issues such as cardiovascular disease or depressive disorders, but also put your body battery in the red and limit your brain's capacity and functioning. You have no energy spare to give to your personal growth goals.

If this is raising a red flag for you, it's your signal that your limits are being tested and you need to lean in and listen to your body. It's time to pause and make adjustments.

When it comes to stress, some things are outside of your control, such as global pandemics, work challenges and health problems. However, you can grab hold of certain things, such as prioritising tasks and laying the right foundations for your physical wellbeing so that you can create capacity. In doing so, you can recharge your own body battery. This is where the physiology basics come in.

The physiology basics

Understanding growth as something our system can only do when it has energy to spare and the right physiological conditions shifts how we think about wellbeing. The physiology basics stop looking like shiny habits and the glossy Instagram version of 'wellness', and start looking more like scaffolding. These basics are the plain, biological foundations your brain and body relies on to function.

In this section, I cover the three elements that physically support your body and brain's energy availability, and your brain's capacity for neuroplastic change. These elements are:

- nutrition
- sleep
- movement.

I'm not going to go too deeply into the 'what' here. Other books are available for that. Instead, my aim is to help you understand that the state of your physical brain and body can either limit or expand your capacity for growth, learning and change, and help you consider the things that are within your control to provide the physiological conditions your body and brain need.

The first foundation I cover is the one most people underestimate, ignore or abandon the moment life gets busy: nutrition. However, research consistently shows that nutrition doesn't just influence your physical health but also changes the way your brain functions, and particularly the systems responsible for learning, memory and emotional regulation. (See, for example, 'The influence of dietary factors in central nervous system plasticity and injury recovery', by Fernando Gomez-Pinilla and Alexis G. Gomez.) Eating more whole, unprocessed foods helps you look after the brain circuits involved in cognitive flexibility, while long periods of poor nutrition reduce the very neurochemicals that support growth. So let's start with ways you can improve your nutrition.

Nutrition: The boring pillar of wellbeing

Nutrition is almost always the first ball we drop when we're in the thick of the juggle, even though we all know better. The reality is when you're stretching yourself in other areas—leading, learning and growing—your capacity to channel too much energy into a fancy eating regime is going to be limited. This is why nutrition works best when it becomes simple, habitual and a little bit boring.

Chloe McLeod is one of Australia's most experienced and sought-after dietitians, having worked for more than a decade with athletes and leaders who need to be at the top of their game. We sat down in an Adelaide Hills cafe for a coffee and a chat so that I could share her insights in this book. The first question I asked her was whether someone could truly reach their potential without paying attention to nutrition. She paused for a moment before saying, 'No. They can get a long way, but nutrition elevates.' You can perform well for a while eating poorly. Plenty of people do. But Chloe then made a strong point: 'You have no idea how much better you could feel and function if you were fuelling properly.'

And the opposite is also true. If nutrition is ignored for too long, the consequences stack up. Chronic stress combined with poor diet is one of the clearest predictors of long-term health issues, particularly heart health. High performers often don't realise the cumulative load they're putting on their bodies until something forces a slowdown. And these chronic health problems impact not only their longevity and quality of life, but also (as already highlighted) their ability to grow.

Nutrition and mental performance

Chloe spoke a lot about how immediate the effect of food is on cognition, focus and emotional stability. As someone who has been described more than once by my husband as 'hangry', I agree.

She sees a pattern in stressed-out high performers who unintentionally starve their brains. Some avoid carbohydrates entirely, some literally forget to eat, some work through back-to-back meetings and only realise at dinner time that they haven't had a proper meal all day.

Chloe explained that your brain burns through glucose faster than any other organ. When blood sugar drops, most people don't experience it as hunger, they experience it as:

- anxiety
- irritability
- brain fog
- emotional volatility
- feeling 'off' without knowing why.

Sound familiar? Chloe shared that when her clients start fuelling more consistently, especially earlier in the day, they notice a change in how calm and stable they are. They thought they were anxious and exhausted, but they were just hungry.

Your experience of this might be that you feel completely on track to follow through with your growth experiments when you wake up in the morning, but by the time you get to the end of the day you've conked out. It's worth considering whether your undesired behaviour is simply about the quality and quantity of the nutrition you're consuming.

Why nutrition is the first ball to drop

Chloe works closely with leaders and executives, and she sees the same pattern over and over again: nutrition is the first ball to drop. This isn't because people don't know it's important, but because of the following:

- They don't have habits deeply ingrained.
- They hit decision fatigue.
- Their environment isn't set up for success.
- They rely on willpower instead of structure.
- They eat reactively instead of intentionally.

This is especially true for people who travel, attend evening events or have unpredictable days. Without systems, you can default to what's fastest and easiest, not what's best. If your fridge is empty, if you get home exhausted, if every work event serves beige food or if UberEats is faster than assembling a meal, your brain will choose the easiest option. It wants to save energy.

Chloe also stressed something that links directly to the previous chapter on environment: nutrition is mostly an environment problem, not a discipline problem. She said, 'Make the healthy choice the easy choice'.

Make nutrition the boring pillar

I sat and listened to Chloe share her experience in working with growth-focused leaders and athletes for about half an hour and, by the end of it, this is the phrase I used to sum it all up: 'Make nutrition the boring pillar.'

Whatever your nutrition philosophy, fuelling your body well needs to be easy for you to do. The more complex your nutrition plan, the less likely you'll be to access the required behaviours when life gets hard.

In real life, boring nutrition looks like:

- simple, repeatable meals
- rotating the same breakfasts and lunches
- using smart convenience (such as meal delivery, pre-cut veg, microwave rice and pre-cooked meats)
- having food available that doesn't require thinking
- outsourcing where needed (taking advantage of an EA, a partner or weekly grocery delivery)
- setting up your home so the healthy choice is the easy choice.

Chloe said a lot of high performers feel shame when they 'drop the ball', and that shame pushes them into all-or-nothing thinking. But once nutrition becomes routine and stabilised, slip-ups stop mattering. A chaotic week doesn't derail you; it just becomes a week.

Sleep: The night shift of growth

Back in chapter 2, I emphasised that just because your brain is capable of changing, that doesn't automatically mean it will. For neuroplastic change to occur, for your brain to integrate the learnings and update itself based on the experiments you're running and the experiences you're having, four conditions need to be present:

1. awareness
2. focused experience
3. reflection
4. consolidation.

Consolidation happens while you sleep. This is the time when your brain takes everything you paid attention to during the day—the friction, the mistakes, the small wins, the effort and the learnings—and decides what's worth wiring in.

A large review of human and animal studies conducted by Jacob Pickersgill and colleagues (and published in *Frontiers in Psychology*), shows that both deep sleep and REM sleep play different roles in helping your brain rewire itself. While deep sleep strengthens the pathways you used during the day, REM sleep helps you process and integrate the emotional meaning behind them. Together, they act like the maintenance crew and the filing system for your brain.

Sleep researchers consistently show that both the *quantity* and the *quality* of sleep matter here. You can be in bed for eight hours and still wake up feeling like a shell of yourself if your sleep was shallow or interrupted. When your sleep cycles don't complete, your brain can't complete its maintenance and filing work. And when consolidation doesn't happen, growth stalls.

In this state, your system reallocates energy to basic survival—as if your brain were saying, 'I don't have enough to stretch today. I'm focusing on keeping the lights on'.

So sleep has a number of functions when it comes to growth, including rest and recovery, consolidation and neuroplastic change, and recharging your energy stores for the coming day. When sleep is inconsistent or shallow, your brain starts the next morning already in low power mode.

Why people struggle with sleep

If you're experiencing more stress than usual, you've got a lot on your mind or you're experiencing significant change (which seems to be most of us much of the time), it's not hard to see why sleep suffers. But let's look at some specific factors that can affect the quantity and quality of your sleep:

- You finally get quiet time at night, so you 'revenge scroll' to reclaim space.
- Screens suppress melatonin and push your natural sleep window later.
- Stress creates that 3 am cortisol spike that jolts you awake.
- Alcohol helps you fall asleep but disrupts your sleep cycles.
- Inconsistent bedtimes mess with your circadian rhythm.
- You go from high-adrenaline work straight into trying to 'switch off', and your nervous system struggles with it.

This is the reality of your body meeting modern life without a system in place to manage it.

The simplest tools for better sleep

You don't need a 20-step routine to prepare yourself for better sleep. Your brain just needs simple cues that help it do what it already knows how to do.

Try the following:

- *Increase morning light:* Get outside within an hour of waking. This anchors your circadian rhythm and improves sleep the next night.
- *Reduce light at night:* Dim the lights and reduce screen exposure. Let your body wind down.
- *Make timing consistent:* A roughly consistent bedtime is enough to help your system prepare.
- *Handle the 3 am wake-up:* Most of the time this is due to cortisol, not crisis. Avoid checking the clock. Slow your breathing. Let your system settle.

- *Reduce alcohol on work nights:* Alcohol helps you fall asleep but disrupts the cycles you need for growth and emotional stability.
- *Create a wind-down signal:* This signal could be a shower, some stretching or reading, or a cup of tea. The content matters less than the consistency.

Movement: Using energy to build energy

Poet Alexander Pope knew the importance of movement before neuroscience even existed when he said, 'Strength of mind is exercise, not rest'.

It sounds counterintuitive to say that using energy through exercise actually helps you build more of it, but perhaps you've experienced this yourself. On the days you're tired, stretched thin or overwhelmed, movement feels like the last thing you have capacity for. Yet if you manage to do it, it's often the thing that helps you feel most like yourself again. Movement is one of the only things that drains your body budget now and increases it later.

When you move your body, whether through a walk, strength training, yoga or gardening, a couple of things happen at once:

1. You're burning energy in the moment, which is why it feels hard to start.
2. You're activating the systems that replenish and grow your long-term energy stores, including your cardiovascular capacity, metabolic flexibility and, importantly for this book, your neuroplasticity.

Exercise has been proven to cause major structural and functional changes in the brain, and particularly in the limbic system, which is the part of your brain responsible for emotional regulation, motivation and memory.

One of the clearest findings in neuroscience is that even brief, moderate movement increases the brain's ability to learn and adapt. It boosts blood flow, oxygen and glucose to the brain, and stimulates the release of the protein brain-derived neurotrophic factor (BDNF), which helps support the growth and strength of neural pathways. Movement literally primes your brain to change.

It's also one of the best tools you have to manage stress. Exercise reduces levels of the body's stress hormones, such as adrenaline and cortisol. It also stimulates the production of endorphins, chemicals in the brain that are the body's natural painkillers and mood elevators. It's kind of like plugging yourself in to recharge.

You don't need to punish yourself in the gym to get these effects, with the research consistently highlighting that anything is better than nothing. Ten minutes counts. A brisk walk counts. Moving your body in a way that feels doable, safe and repeatable counts. Your aim isn't to become an athlete, but to give your brain and body the conditions they need to support the growth you're trying to create.

Accepting the stage you're in

I was recently discussing the physiology lever in a workshop with a group of banking leaders. When people started sharing their tools for managing their body batteries, a lady put her hand up. She was feeling frustrated, because many in the room were sharing their morning routines and evening wind downs, and she had an 18-month-old child. If she tried to implement a routine like those being suggested, it would be constantly interrupted and it just didn't feel possible.

I also work a great deal with women who are in their perimenopause and menopause stages of life, and understand that what worked for them in their 30s isn't cutting it for them anymore. Men can experience hormonal changes as well, with a gradual decrease in testosterone potentially impacting mood, energy and cognition. Hormonal influences play a significant role in shaping neuroplasticity, energy and general wellbeing. Your physiological foundations are going to look different during different periods of your life.

This is important to note. Any change, any routine, any experiment needs to be considered in your unique context. This pillar, like any other change, needs to be managed with the N-of-1 approach outlined in chapter 3. What I can manage to make stick in my life will be different from what works for you. And what you can do now will likely be different to what you can do in five years.

Honour the period you're in.

Micro-experiment: Physiology audit

Like in the environment lever from the previous chapter, you can begin with a simple audit, in this case of your body battery, and use this audit to design your micro-experiments for sleep, nutrition and movement.

One of the best and simplest tools I've found to gather some initial data on your battery expanders, sustainers and drainers is the body battery diagram provided here. Use this image to consider your life's stressors, as well as the foods you eat, your sleep routines and your exercise habits. Note down anything that charges your battery—you can either draw a battery and note these aspects above it, similar to the figure shown, or simply write a list. Next, note anything that drains the battery, including them below the battery you've drawn or in a separate list. Remember to also include any feelings of boredom or lack of stimulation that may also be draining your battery.

Note any sustainers, those habits that ground you and keep you level, through the middle of the battery or in another list.

Allow these notes to form the basis of your physiology lever experiments.

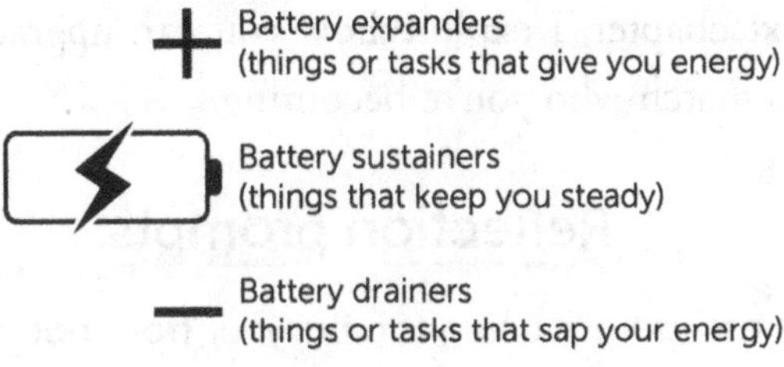

The energy to become who you're becoming

Looking back on my own 2020, it wasn't my ambition that disappeared, or my capability or drive. I was just at capacity. My battery was drained. Growth hadn't become impossible, but for that moment in time it was biologically unrealistic. My energy was needed elsewhere.

And that's true for all of us. During times of high metabolic load, chronic stress, young kids and ageing parents, your physiology and your capacity sets the limits of what you can ask of yourself. But it also holds the potential for what you can become.

When you tend to your physiological foundations of nutrition, sleep and movement, not perfectly, just consistently, you give your brain more of the energy and the raw materials it needs to stretch.

But you know that energy alone isn't enough. Physiology is only one of the three levers for growth. You can no doubt think of someone who is physically well but mentally stuck; someone who seems to be placed in the world surrounded by opportunity, but who doesn't seem able to grab it with both hands. Perhaps that person is you. This can happen because your capacity for growth is shaped by your psychology as well. If your beliefs and your identity don't line up with where you want to go, you're going to feel like you're getting in your own way.

Physiology supports your capacity. Psychology shapes your possibility.

In the next chapter, I explore how you can upgrade your identity and beliefs to match who you're becoming.

Reflection prompts

◆ Are you stressed from being too busy, or from not being busy enough? Or are you busy with the wrong things?

◆ What do you eat when you realise you've forgotten to eat? What does that pattern tell you about your environment setup?

◆ What are you doing in the hour before bed that your brain might be reading as 'stay awake' signals?

◆ What stops you from moving when you're tired? Is it actually a lack of energy, or something else?

◆ Are you trying to force a routine that doesn't fit your current life? Why?

◆ Looking at your body battery audit, what's one thing you could test this week that might add more charge than it costs?

6

Psychology

Professor Kevin Cokley is one of the world's leading experts on self-doubt. He has spent decades studying the imposter phenomenon, teaching it, publishing research on it and speaking about it globally. He has quite literally written the book on it (appropriately titled *The Imposter Phenomenon*).

One day, I was driving to an appointment and listening to Kevin speak to Shankar Vedantam on the *Hidden Brain* podcast. They were chatting about the psychology of self-doubt when Professor Cokley dropped a bomb that almost made me choke on my coffee. Despite being one of the most cited psychologists in his field, Professor Cokley googles himself daily to remind himself that he deserves the accolades he receives.

Each day, he looks at his publication list, checks how many times his research has been cited and scans his metrics. The numbers barely change from one day to the next, but he keeps going back to them. He said he does this to remind himself that the recognition he receives is real, that people value his work for a reason and that he has earned his place. He is the world leading expert on the imposter phenomenon, and he feels all 'impostery' about it.

If ever there was a moment in this book that really drives home that your answer for personal growth isn't going to come from your next course or personal development book, let it be this one. Knowing a load of information doesn't help you nail it. You can hold a PhD on the imposter phenomenon and still feel like an imposter.

That's why this isn't a psychology book, but an action book. Simply learning about psychology doesn't cure self-doubt. But it is important to understand psychology as another significant lever for growth you can pull. As with your environment (covered in chapter 4) and your physiology (chapter 5), your psychology is either supporting who you want to become or hindering it.

To illustrate this, let me use the same example I used when running a workshop in Perth for a group of small business owners. I was talking through the three levers, environment, physiology and psychology, when a man who I'd shared a bit of banter with throughout the morning called out, 'You've drawn these levers as equal in size, but obviously your psychology, your mindset, is going to impact you more than your environment or your physiology'.

I said, 'Tell that to someone growing up in poverty or battling cancer.'

The room went quiet, and then the man laughed and said 'fair point'.

Perhaps that was a bit harsh, but of course the answer to which lever is the most influential is 'it depends'.

Most of the individuals and teams I work with are stressed but otherwise well, and they've got a secure roof over their heads. But sometimes they're trying to operate within a workplace culture or sometimes even a relationship that doesn't align with the life they want, and sometimes they really are so stressed and tired that they're in constant survival mode and we need to focus our experiments there first.

But, as my friend in Perth pointed out, mindset, beliefs and identity do really matter. They can cause a great deal of pain, prevent you from taking action in the direction of your goals, and stop you from ever truly being able to enjoy and experience your own success.

When your psychology lever is out of alignment, it usually shows up in one of the following three complaints:

1. 'I know what I want but I keep self-sabotaging.'
2. 'I know what I want but I'm not sure if I can do it.'
3. 'I've achieved what I want but I feel like an imposter. People think I know what I'm doing, but I'm actually just winging it.'

In this chapter, I run through why these experiences are so convincing, why they happen even when life looks good on the outside, and how to work with them rather than battling them. This chapter allows you to run your experiments without retreating, hiding or draining your energy trying to overcome yourself.

But, first, let me give it to you straight. Self-sabotage doesn't exist. And, yes, you are an imposter. If you're doing something you've never done before and expecting to feel like an expert, this is where you'll live. The uncertainty of stretching into something new is uncomfortable. That discomfort has a purpose.

Now, I know you don't believe me yet. You're thinking about the time you procrastinated on the big project, hit snooze on your alarm, said no to a stretch opportunity or avoided a conversation that then spiralled into something bigger than it needed to be. You might be thinking: *That was definitely self-sabotage. I got in my own way.*

But that's not how it works. Let me show you.

Self-sabotage is a myth

Sophie had an idea for a product-based startup. She was clever, driven and capable, and her idea really had legs. The problem was that she was a physio by trade and, although the product was in her area of expertise, she had no idea how to build an e-commerce business. So she did what a lot of smart people do when they want to try something new: she found some books and courses. (She bought 15 online courses, in fact.) Bookmarked in her browser were pages on 'Shopify mastery' and 'TikTok for beginners', along with information on product photography and copywriting. She'd spent thousands of dollars and spent hours on YouTube, but she'd implemented nothing.

Sophie is the type of person who is used to succeeding. She's whip smart, played high-level sport, has strong relationships and a great career. She knew what it took to be successful in these areas, and it had become second nature to her. But this project felt different. She didn't have a rule book, she didn't have the credentials, she'd never done anything like it before and she had no proof she could do it.

Counterintuitively, it's high achievers who often struggle most with this. When you're used to succeeding, uncertainty feels more threatening. Your brain has learned to avoid situations where you might fail, and you get really good at rationalising yourself out of things. Your intelligence can become a liability. And avoiding the 'threat' of failure was all that Sophie's brain was doing. It was protecting her from the unfamiliar possibility of being bad at something.

When Sophie came to me for coaching, I suspected she was treating me like course number 16. Coaching was another way for her to feel like she was progressing without having to actually step into the arena. She told me what she wanted to build and I asked her what was stopping her. She said, 'I keep self-sabotaging. I have all the information I need, but I just can't get the job done'. I asked her what would happen if she launched the product tomorrow, and she cringed. 'I can't. I don't know how to do Facebook ads and no-one will see it.'

'What if you didn't run Facebook ads?'

'How would anyone find it?'

'What if you just told ten friends?'

Pause. 'That's not how you're supposed to launch a business.'

'Says who?'

'Every course I've bought.'

Sophie truly felt like she was getting in her own way and undermining her own goals, as if a part of her secretly wanted her to fail. But she wasn't self-sabotaging; she was self-protecting. If she actually launched, she would run out of excuses and have to front up to the potential that her idea might not work. As long as she stayed in 'learning mode', her dream, and her identity, stayed safe.

This is what people get wrong when they think about self-sabotage. The brain doesn't work that way. It's not trying to stitch you up; it just doesn't care so much for your growth goals. The goal of your brain is to protect you, not make your dreams come true.

So when something feels like a threat, your brain has some tricks up its sleeve to rescue you.

Avoidance: Self-protection rather than self-sabotage

Psychologists Fuschia Sirois and Tim Pychyl, two of the world's leading procrastination researchers, call avoidance an 'emotion regulation strategy'. Rather than procrastination being a motivation or discipline problem, they argue it is a short-term mood-repair solution.

You often don't avoid a task because you're lazy. You avoid it because, for a moment at least, it makes you feel better. It soothes anxiety, reduces uncertainty and makes you feel calmer.

I've outlined in previous chapters why change and growth can feel hard. Your brain likes certainty, and feeling certain when you're doing something you've never done before is hard. So you do something easier instead. You watch another YouTube tutorial, you reorganise your inbox, you research Facebook ads and, as a result, you feel better for a little while. Your brain, with the best of intentions, comes to the rescue with avoidance as a solution to your discomfort problem.

Addiction, one of the most destructive behaviours we see, works this way as well. Like avoidance, it's not 'the problem'. It's the solution to a problem. It's a coping strategy that works, until it doesn't.

The same is true for procrastination, over-preparing, hesitating or retreating. They're behaviours you do to keep yourself safe. Instead of sabotage, they're short-term emotion regulation strategies for protection.

But sometimes the threat runs deeper than temporary discomfort. Sometimes the behaviour you want to repeat requires you to show up as someone you don't yet see yourself as.

Identity threat

A threat to your identity makes the self-protection and avoidance tendency even stronger. The more something threatens your identity, the more you will avoid it. If making a change requires you to change your own view of yourself—for example, how successful you think you are, whether you're the kind of person who wins or loses, or the kind of values you uphold—the more resistance you're going to feel and the bigger your inner struggle.

A certain comfort comes with knowing your place in the world. Anything that messes with that is going to feel risky, even if it could make your life better.

This is why people are often just as afraid of success as they are of failure, even if they're not aware of it. Scaling your side gig to six figures could threaten your identity as much as being made redundant. Losing 30 kilograms could threaten your identity as much as gaining it. Both require you to become someone new. Both force you to update the story you've been telling yourself about who you are.

For Sophie, staying stuck in learning mode wasn't just about soothing the anxiety of launching; it was about preserving her identity as the type of person who succeeds. If she launched and it flopped, she'd have to reckon with the idea that maybe she wasn't as capable as she thought. If she launched and it worked, she'd have to become the kind of person who runs a business.

Either way, her identity was under threat, so her brain kept her safe by keeping her stuck.

How experiments lower the stakes

Of course, Sophie didn't know all this yet, so she genuinely was trying to move forward. She thought that if she just had all the answers she'd be able to get things moving (hence, all the courses). Capability building, strategy sessions, relentless planning are all noble pursuits. But they're treating the symptom without addressing the cause—which is the gap between who you are and who you're being asked to become.

In his book *Solving the Procrastination Puzzle*, Pychyl says the way through is just getting started. Once we get started on a task, we tend to view it much less negatively than when we are actively avoiding it. Before we get started, we dread the task. After starting, we realise it's not that bad. We gain a feeling of momentum, and we feel better about ourselves for getting something done.

The Experiment Mindset is built for this. It's designed to lower the stakes so you can get started. You're not 'launching a business'; you're simply testing whether anyone wants the product you're selling. You're not 'becoming a speaker'; you're learning what techniques work to keep you from freezing on stage. The experiment gives you permission to try without having to immediately update your entire identity.

Once you're started, you gain a sense of agency and momentum and the dread drops away. Sometimes the evidence you gather is enough to start upgrading your identity in itself. Of course, you're not going to feel like the type of person who runs a startup until you're a person who runs a startup.

I asked Sophie the following: 'What if you stopped trying to launch a business and started trying to find out if anyone actually wants this thing?' I wanted to know what the smallest possible version of her product launch would look like. What was her minimum viable experiment? How could we gather some data? Sophie had already ordered some product and had it sitting in a box at home. So she decided to take them to work and offer them to her physiotherapy clients.

Two weeks later, Sophie messaged me to let me know she'd sold out. One client she'd offered the product to had posted about it on Instagram, and two strangers had come to the reception desk asking where they could get one.

'How do you feel?' I asked when we spoke next.

'Terrified', she laughed. 'But also ... like I can actually do this.'

She'd gathered some data and started to prove the concept. More importantly, and she'd started to see herself as the type of person who launches products.

This kind of breakthrough can provide excellent progress, but if you've got more work to be done within the psychology lever, it won't always get you all the way there.

What happens after you take the first step

What happens next can go one of three ways.

1. *The experiment works and you keep going:* You gather your data and run your next experiment, iterating and evolving. Happy days, because the psychology lever isn't an inhibitor.

2. *The experiment works but you don't keep going:* You get results and prove the thing is possible, but then you stop. You fall back to baseline (or the hedonic set point discussed in chapter 1). You tell yourself that you were just testing and you're not

ready to really commit yet. You go back to planning mode, or focus on something else for a while. This is the person who sells out their first batch of product, and then spends the next six months 'researching suppliers' instead of making the next batch. Or the leader who runs a successful team workshop, and then goes back to doing everything themselves.

3. *The experiment works and you keep going—but:* You spend the entire time terrified, convinced you're winging it. You're sure that, any moment now, someone's going to figure out you don't belong here. You're performing on the outside, but on the inside you feel like a fraud.

Options two and three have the same underlying mechanism: the behaviour changed, but the identity didn't. That's why Sophie felt like she could do it, but still felt terrified. The fear you feel when doing something new is not a sign you shouldn't do it. It's a signal your identity hasn't caught up yet. When your vision levels up and your behaviours shift, your identity needs to upgrade too. Otherwise, you'll either fall back to baseline or keep going and feel like rubbish.

Let's take a look at how to close the gap.

Upgrading your identity

Back in chapter 3, I asked you to set your horizon—to get clear on who you want to become, not just what you want to achieve. But knowing who you want to become isn't the same as actually becoming that person.

If the gap between your current identity and your future identity is too wide, your brain will keep pulling you back to what's familiar. You'll fall into option 2 from the preceding list (retreat to baseline) or option 3 (keep going but feel like a fraud).

So how do you actually close the gap? The Experiment Mindset is designed to do a lot of this work for you. Every time you run an experiment and gather evidence that you can do the thing, you're updating your identity in real time. Small experiments create small identity shifts and, over time, those shifts compound.

But sometimes you need more than evidence. Sometimes you need to actively interrogate the story you're telling yourself about who you are and who you think you need to be.

Why you feel like an imposter

Much of my early work focused on imposter syndrome, largely because I wanted to solve it for myself. What I've learned after working with hundreds of clients over nine years is this: imposter syndrome isn't a bug; it's a feature.

If you're feeling like an imposter, you're comparing your current identity to the identity you think you need to have to do what you're doing. And they don't match. So you've drawn one or all of the following conclusions:

- 'I'm not qualified to be here.'
- 'I'm faking it.'
- 'Someone's going to figure me out.'

But it's unlikely that's what is actually happening. What's happening is that your mind is comparing two things:

1. Who you think you are right now.
2. Who you think you need to be to do this job.

And when those two images don't line up, it's flagged as a very real threat. *You're literally an imposter in your own mind.*

When you have these imposter feelings, I recommend you embrace it or bust it (or both). The first one is simple.

Embrace the imposter

I still experience self-doubt and imposter syndrome. Like Professor Cokley, just because I'm writing the book on personal growth doesn't mean I find it easy. But it's not meant to be.

A couple of years ago I was invited to be a keynote speaker at a global workplace health and safety conference in Melbourne. I arrived early to hear the other speakers, settling in with a few hundred delegates as the MC began his opening remarks.

The list of keynote speakers came up on the screen, along with our photos and titles, one by one. My palms started sweating, my heart was racing, and I felt like I had a spotlight on me, with the entire room thinking, *What on earth is she doing here?*

The list of speakers included the following:

- the Director of the NASA Safety Center
- a German professor
- the Commissioner of Resilience NSW
- Australia's first-ever female navy helicopter pilot
- an Antarctic expedition leader
- little old me.

I was terrified. Did I feel like I belonged there? Absolutely bloody not. Did I cheat and lie to get myself there? Absolutely bloody not.

I was invited because I had built a reputation as an excellent speaker who could engage an audience and shift minds. I felt like an imposter because I was operating at a level I hadn't hit before, and that feeling wasn't wrong. It was normal, even expected. Okay.

These days, I experience the imposter feelings as a sign that I'm stretching myself. It's exciting. I'm giving something new a try, and I'm going to learn from it whether it's successful or not. There is no losing. This is what I encourage you to do too.

If you're not ready to do that yet, I've designed a tool for that.

Bust the imposter

I've connected with thousands of leaders, professionals and generally successful humans in my career, and I've only met one who hadn't experienced some form of imposter feelings in their lifetime. I've needed to upgrade my identity in my own mind over and over again to get to where I am. Imposter syndrome is something I've worked on myself, and something I've worked on with hundreds of coaching clients over nine years.

The pattern is the same. Who they think they are, their current identity, and who they think they need to be in order to be where they're going don't line up.

The tool I've created to combat these feelings does two things. First, it helps you get clear on the reality of your current identity, and understand that your self-perception isn't always an accurate reflection of who you really are. Secondly, it helps you get clear on who you think you need to be.

When I was a young leader, my imposter feelings were debilitating. I was so scared of walking into work that I would physically shrink as I walked through those doors.

During this time, I was leading the build of a new medical imaging clinic, and one day I went on site to check the progress. I met with the building supervisor, popped my hard hat on and walked through, feeling excited to have a look. When the supervisor introduced me to his workers, he said, 'This is the boss!' And they all laughed. A 20-something blonde woman wasn't the picture of a 'boss' they had in mind. I couldn't control what they expected, but really what was going on in the room wasn't much different to what was going on in my own head. And I could control that.

Who was I picturing when I thought of who I needed to be to do my job? I was thinking of my boss—a 50-year-old man with 30 years of management experience, an accounting background and an MBA.

For as long as that was who I thought I needed to be, I would be an imposter. It wasn't ever going to happen.

I wish I had asked myself, 'Who do I actually need to be to do this job well?' Not my boss, not some idealised version of a leader, just me, with all of my strengths and gaps, growing into a role I'd never done before.

That's the second step in my Imposter Buster tool. To consider who you actually need to be in order to do your job well. It's normal to have capability gaps when you stretch yourself, since you learn through doing it. So don't stuff those gaps away; instead, write them down and use them to create your development plan. Make those your experiments to run.

Tool: The Imposter Buster

Imposter feelings almost always show up when two images don't match:

1. How you see yourself now.
2. Who you think you 'should' be to deserve your role or opportunity.

This tool helps you see both clearly, and turn the gap into a development plan instead of a reason to torture yourself.

Grab your journal and follow along.

Step 1: Set the context

Think of a specific situation where you feel like an imposter—for example, when presenting to the executive team, leading a more experienced team or pitching to investors. Write these situations down.

(continued)

Step 2: Map the two identities

Draw a table similar to the one provided in your journal and fill it in as honestly as you can.

In the 'How I see myself' column, write down your current self-perception in this context. In the 'Who I think I should be' column, include the person you're holding yourself up against. This might be a current or former boss or mentor, or an imaginary 'perfect leader'. If a real person, it's okay to name them.

How I see myself	Who I think I should be
Experience	
Knowledge	
Strengths	
Style/personality	
Credentials	

Step 3: Reflection

Now work through these prompts:

1. 'Where am I underestimating myself?'
   - This is about what strengths, experience or evidence you may have downplayed or ignored.
   - Consider asking a trusted colleague or friend for their view.
   - Look at past feedback, performance reviews or strengths surveys.
2. 'Where is "imagined me" unrealistic or unnecessary?'
   - Is it literally impossible for you to match this image? Consider, for example, your age and lived experience.
   - Do you actually need what you've imagined—for example, 30 years' experience and an MBA—to do this job well?

3. 'Where do genuine, normal capability gaps exist?' Break these down into:
   ◆ skills you can learn
   ◆ knowledge you can build
   ◆ experience you can only get by doing the role.

These gaps are not reasons you don't belong; they provide your growth plan.

Now, instead of an invisible list of worries in your head, you're looking at the reality on paper. What can you do now to accept where you are, and move toward where you want to be?

What about limiting beliefs?

Sometimes what blocks you isn't your behaviour or your identity, but a belief you formed years ago that no longer fits who you're becoming.

Beliefs are predictions your brain made based on old data—and often very old data. This data could have come from childhood experiences, early feedback, a single failure that felt big at the time, subtle messages from the environments you grew up in or sometimes a big defining moment that is a bit more fresh. These moments become shortcuts your brain uses to make sense of the world.

Sometimes these beliefs can be resourceful and helpful, like 'I believe I can figure things out', and sometimes they can be limiting. Limiting beliefs often sound like:

- 'I'm not the type of person who ...'
- 'I could never ...'
- 'People like me don't ...'

They feel true because they're familiar, not because they're accurate.

The problem is that once a belief is formed, your mind gets good at finding evidence to confirm it and ignoring the evidence that contradicts it. Psychologists call this 'confirmation bias'. You might run a successful experiment, gather proof you can do the thing, and still say, 'That was a fluke' because your brain is protecting an old belief.

The good news is that beliefs are workable. You don't need to reverse every thought or experience you've ever had through years of therapy or rewrite your entire story. You just need to treat your beliefs as hypotheses instead of instructions. In this way, they become something to test, rather than something to obey.

And I can offer two simple ways to do that.

A future-focused belief experiment

This is the Experiment Mindset at its simplest. Take a belief that might be blocking your growth and run a small experiment that directly tests it. For example:

- 'I'm terrible at public speaking.' Give a five-minute update to three colleagues.
- 'I'm not creative.' Create something just for fun and see what happens.
- 'I fall apart under pressure.' Set a timer and practise working with urgency.

You're not trying to prove yourself wrong or shatter your belief system; you're just gathering fresh data. And this data adds up.

A retrospective belief experiment

If acting forward with a future-focused experiment feels too big, or isn't doing the trick, try looking backwards instead. Ask yourself:

- 'When did I first learn this about myself? What else could that moment have meant?'
- 'If I witnessed that same moment happening to someone else, what would I believe about them?'

Most people realise the belief came from a single moment, a single comment or an outdated version of themselves. Just identifying the origin point can be enough to break the illusion that the belief is a universal truth. I wonder what you'd think if you went back and experienced that same event with all that you know now.

Micro-experiment: Psychology audit

What's one belief you hold about yourself that might just be old data? What tiny experiment could help you gather new data?

Limiting beliefs are predictions your brain made based on old data. Experiments, whether retrospective or prospective, provide new data, and new data can update old beliefs. The same goes for imposter syndrome.

Auditing your beliefs in this way is exactly what a growth-oriented mind does. You can treat your identity and your beliefs as something flexible, examinable and upgradable. In this way, you're preparing yourself for stepping out into the world and living with an Experiment Mindset.

From here on, the meaning you attach to your experiences—that is, your mindset—shapes your reality and keeps you flexible.

Mindset matters

While your brain's main job is to keep you safe and alive, your mind's job is to help you make sense of the world. The moment you come up against a setback, hurdle, win or opportunity to stretch, your mind assigns it a meaning. That meaning's going to determine whether you expand, retreat, learn or freeze. This meaning-making system is your mindset—and this is where this chapter all comes together.

Mindset is the *lens* your brain uses to interpret experience based on a set of beliefs or assumptions about that thing. This entire book is designed to help you internalise a mindset—a deep understanding of the science of growth and an integrated set of associated beliefs and tools that help you to actually grow.

Director of Stanford's Mind and Body Lab, Associate Professor Alia Crum, has spent her career on this. Her research consistently shows that mindset is so much more than just a perspective. It directly influences your physiology, behaviour and long-term growth. What she's found through her work is striking.

Mindset doesn't just change how you think; it changes what your brain and body believe is possible. This matters for your growth because your experiments don't unfold in a vacuum. You bring your mindset to every one of them.

Let me share one of Professor Crum's most compelling stories so that you can see how powerful this is.

Professor Alia Crum's research: When mindset changes your biology

Some of Crum's most compelling research on mindset is in the area of stress mindsets. Essentially, this research asked, 'If you change how people think about stress, does their body respond differently?'

To find out, Crum and her colleagues ran a series of experiments in which they didn't change people's workload, their deadlines or their bosses. They changed only the story people were told about stress.

First, they randomly assigned participants into two groups:

◆ Group one watched a video that framed stress as harmful—something that damages your health, performance and safety.

◆ Group two watched a video that framed stress as helpful—something that can sharpen focus, increase alertness and boost performance.

Both videos were grounded in real research. Stress can be harmful and it can be helpful, as covered in the previous chapter. The videos were designed to prime two different mindsets: 'stress is debilitating' versus 'stress is enhancing'.

After the video, everyone faced the same stressful task.

While all of this was happening, the researchers took saliva samples to track two key hormones:

◆ *Cortisol:* The classic stress hormone. It mobilises energy by turning stored sugar and fat into fuel and temporarily putting non-essential systems such as digestion and reproduction on the backburner.

◆ *DHEA:* An anabolic 'growth' hormone and neurosteroid. It helps the brain learn from stress, supports neural growth, and offsets some of cortisol's wear-and-tear effects. It's been linked to better recovery, lower risk of anxiety and depression, and improved long-term health.

(continued)

Both hormones are important, and neither is good or bad on its own. What matters is the ratio between them.

Researchers call the ratio of DHEA to cortisol the 'growth index' of a stress response. A higher growth index (more DHEA relative to cortisol) is associated with people who flourish under stress—they recover faster, show more resilience and are less likely to suffer the long-term health costs of chronic stress.

Back to the experiment—and the findings were incredible:

◆ Watching the preceding videos didn't make stress disappear. Both groups still felt stressed when completing the required task, and cortisol still went up for everyone during the stressful task.

◆ The difference was seen in those who had been primed to see stress as enhancing. These participants produced more DHEA and, therefore, had a higher growth index than those primed to see stress as harmful.

Same stressful task, same spike in cortisol. The only difference was the mindset people brought into the room, and that was enough to shift their body into a more growth-oriented stress response.

In other words, viewing stress as potentially helpful didn't make it disappear. The mindset physically changed what their stress did for them.

Maybe it's starting to land why I keep encouraging you to learn to love the struggle.

More good news: Mindset shifts don't just work once

Crum next took her work out of the lab and into a workplace with employees in a large financial organisation. In this experiment, participants completed brief 'rethink stress' training over about a week, including short videos and exercises. This training:

- educated them about the idea that stress can have enhancing as well as harmful effects
- asked them to apply this mindset to their own current stressors
- invited them to share what they'd learned with others.

What Crum and her fellow researchers found is important for your growth experiments:

- People who shifted toward a 'stress can be enhancing' mindset didn't report less stress. Their lives didn't magically become easier.
- They did report better health and wellbeing, and fewer physical symptoms of stress. They also showed better work performance than those who stayed in the 'stress is harmful' mindset.
- Importantly, these changes lasted beyond the initial training. The new mindset didn't just help them through one mock interview, but also altered how they related to stress in the real world in the weeks that followed.

Changing your mindset doesn't stop tough things from happening, but it does influence whether you shut down and avoid, or lean in and adapt.

When you see stress as purely harmful, you're more likely to:

- become anxious about feeling stressed at all
- distract or numb yourself (using food, alcohol or endless scrolling)
- focus on getting rid of the feelings instead of addressing the source.

When you see stress as something that can be useful, you're more likely to:

- accept the stress response as a sign you care
- plan a strategy for dealing with what's hard
- seek support, feedback or resources
- treat stressful situations as chances to grow skills or strengthen resilience.

Crum calls mindset a *catalyst*. It doesn't fix everything on its own, but it sets off a chain of thoughts, feelings and actions that compound over time.

With the Experiment Mindset you're not pretending that struggling against something new feels good. You're learning to interpret it as information: 'This is hard because it's new and I'm growing. What can I learn from this?'

From here, everything covered in this chapter comes together:

- *Identity asks:* 'Who am I?'
- *Beliefs ask:* 'What's possible for me?'
- *Mindset asks:* 'What does this experience mean?'

When those three are aligned with an Experiment Mindset, stress stops being a reason to retreat and becomes a signal that you're exactly where growth happens.

Reflection prompts

◆ *On self-protection (not self-sabotage):* What are you protecting yourself from by staying stuck where you are?

◆ *On imposter feelings:* Are you feeling like an imposter because you're actually unqualified, or because you're stretching into someone new?

◆ *On limiting beliefs:* What belief are you treating like a fact when it's actually just a hypothesis you've never tested?

◆ *On mindset:* When you feel stressed, do you think, *This is breaking me* or *This is building me*?

The three levers in the growth system

In my late teens, I was unhealthy and overweight. I was working part-time as a fitness instructor at a boutique women's specialist gym while I went through university, but I would spend weekends partying, sometimes on Thursday, Friday and Saturday nights, and then Sundays lazing around, soothing the hangover with comfort food.

Before Instagram and YouTube there were magazines. Remember those? Every month, I would buy *Women's Fitness and Health* magazine. I cared about health and fitness, I'd studied it, it was a passion of mine, and I so badly wanted my behaviours to catch up with my goals.

Every issue included a '12-week body transformation' promotion. You bought the magazine, signed up to the promotion, started on an intense, restricted diet and exercise regime, and took 'before' and 'after' shots to prove your progress. Pages were dedicated to 'before' photos of women holding a newspaper to prove their start date, looking as miserable as you'd expect standing in your undies for a 'before' shot, alongside their glowing, six-packed, smiling 'after' shots, complete with new matching bikini. I didn't make it that far; in fact, I never made it past the first month.

I'd start well: chicken breast and broccoli stacked in the fridge, gym bag by the door, daily workouts locked in. But within weeks, I'd be back on the couch on a Sunday, downing Doritos. What I didn't know then is that I could have run all the experiments I wanted in nutrition and exercise, but they were never going to stick because two other significant influencing factors—or two levers for change—needed upgrading. These were my environment and my psychology. This is how the system works.

In this part of the book, you've met the three levers for growth:

1. *Environment:* The people, places and prompts that surround you.
2. *Physiology:* Your body energy budget, and its foundations in your sleep, movement and nutrition.
3. *Psychology:* Your identity, beliefs and mindset.

These levers are all in constant conversation:

◆ Your environment shapes your behaviours.
◆ Your physiology sets the limits of your capacity.
◆ Your psychology decides what you believe is possible, and what
  you try next.

You've seen that:

◆ what looks like self-sabotage is actually self-protection
◆ imposter feelings are a sign your identity is stretching, not that
  you're a fraud
◆ limiting beliefs are old predictions, not permanent truths
◆ the way you interpret stress can shift your body into survival mode
  or growth mode.

Most importantly, you've seen how to practise a different way of relating
to yourself and the world around you, treating your stories, beliefs and
reactions as data you can work with, not fixed verdicts on who you are.

Now that you know what levers you're working with, you're going to
learn how to actually run your experiments so that you can pull these
levers in a way that expands who you are, not just what you're doing.

Reflection prompt

◆ Of the three levers—environment, physiology or and psychology—
  which one is the limiter to your growth goals right now? What's
  one tiny experiment you're willing to run with that lever this week?

PART III
The Experiment Mindset method

The chapters in the previous parts have outlined how growth works and which levers you may need to pull. Now it's time to actually pull them. Change is an action-based process. You can't think, plan, read or strategise your way there; you've got to *do* something. Plenty of people don't. They set perfect goals, craft beautiful vision boards, gather all the information and then never take the first step. Or they start, it gets hard and they stop.

The Experiment Mindset method is designed to fix that. This book is not a framework but a mindset. The chapters in this part will help you practise until experimentation becomes instinctive. At first, this approach will sit front of mind. Over time, it'll wire into your operating system and become part of who you are.

Frameworks are nice, but a change in mindset can change a life.

You'll learn how to design experiments that are big enough to matter but small enough that you'll actually start. You'll discover how to turn raw data from your life into wisdom you can trust, and how to handle the inevitable moments when things don't go to plan, when the experiment fails or the feedback stings or you want to quit.

Ready?

7
Designing your experiments

A couple of years ago I had a phone call from a woman named Margot who wanted to pick my brains. She was a senior executive in finance and she wanted to do what I'd done—that is, step out of her corporate role and start her own thing. Her goal was to develop a personal development business specifically for professional women, including an online membership platform.

My advice to her was that she needed to stop over-planning and overthinking, and simply get in front of her target audience. I suggested she could run some 'lunch and learns', take a specific group of women out for coffee or do a survey. Basically, she could consider what minimum viable offering she could launch with, so that she could test her concept and gather some data. She didn't take my advice.

Instead, she invested in a $5000 business coaching program, in which she created a vision and a strategy to achieve her goal. She invested $4000 to get her brand and logo created. She spent $3000 in branding photography to create beautiful visual assets so that her website, social media and online platform looked stunning. Another $10 000 went to a PR company to get her into the media so that she could raise her profile and become more visible. And $8000 went to getting her website and online platform built.

The end result looked absolutely first class—stunning and highly professional.

The problem was that nobody wanted to buy it. She took huge action based on absolutely no data, and it cost her not only thousands, and a heap of time, but also her confidence and her momentum. This is the trap of traditional goal setting: it rewards execution over exploration, often requiring you to commit before you collect evidence.

When you chase end goals instead of data, three things tend to happen:

1. You double-down on the wrong thing. The sunk-cost fallacy keeps you trapped in work that isn't working.
2. You beat yourself up. You miss the mark and label it failure instead of feedback.
3. You disengage. Either the goal feels too big to start or too small to care, and it fades off into the background.

Having an Experiment Mindset ends that madness and shifts you from performance to practice. It takes you from 'How do I achieve this?' to 'What can I learn next?' It encourages a sense of agency and momentum that is perpetual. You don't fail; you learn.

The problem with SMART goals

Margot was following a traditional goal-setting path, and she had a clear roadmap to execute. Her goal was SMART:

- *Specific:* 'I want to build a successful personal development business for professional women, including an online membership platform that supports their growth and wellbeing.'
- *Measurable:* 'I'll launch my website and platform within six months, gain 1000 social-media followers and enrol at least 50 paying members in the first three months after launch.'

- *Achievable:* 'I'll invest in professional branding, photography, PR and website development to ensure the business looks credible and attracts my ideal clients.'
- *Relevant:* 'Building this business will allow me to leave my corporate job, create impact for women and establish financial independence.'
- *Time-bound:* 'I'll have my business fully launched and operational by December this year.'

Margot's was a textbook SMART goal, seemingly ticking all of the required boxes to get her to where she wanted to go.

Working through that process must have felt exciting, being ready to go live and deliver it to the world. Hitting 'go' and getting crickets, however, must have felt soul destroying. Unfortunately, this is what happens when you optimise the plan instead of testing the problem. It's heartbreaking because Margot was capable of delivering on her overall goal, but she'd gone about it backwards.

If Margot had approached this with an Experiment Mindset, rather than the linear one she'd used to climb the corporate ladder, things would have gone differently. She would have come out the other side with more insight, more confidence and more self-efficacy—not to mention a much healthier bank balance.

The Experiment Mindset method

Where SMART goals are about the end game, the Experiment Mindset is about the process. SMART goals have their place in project management and execution, but when you're testing something new, when uncertainty is high and learning is the goal, you need a different approach. Unlike traditional goal-setting methods, experiments aren't a win or lose; instead, they're a method of enquiry. When you craft an experiment, you're taking action in order to see where that action leads. The goal is the insight that can tell you where to go next.

I wish I had a sexy acronym to give you, or a step by step, linear process you could follow to get this mindset just right. I don't. What I do have is a set of principles that come together to help you progress along the right path, all while becoming wiser and more informed, with real and relevant data.

You can actually run three types of experiments, and often you'll end up running all three as you move toward a shift in your behaviours or sense of identity. The three types are organic, exploratory and experimental, and they work together as an experiment scale.

The experiment scale

Here's a quick run-through of each of the three types of experiments:

- *Organic—I noticed:* This is where you look back and notice what has happened organically in the past. For Margot, this process might have looked like considering her career and life and what she had tried in personal development, and then noticing what worked and what didn't.
- *Exploratory—I wonder:* This is where you dabble and learn. You're asking yourself open-ended questions, hypothesis testing and gathering some early data. For Margot, this was my early recommendation. She could ask some questions, run some workshops, find out what the pain points are for the women she wanted to serve, or start a blog or an email newsletter. It's low-risk testing. The common trap with these types of experiments, however, is getting stuck here. It's tempting to feel like you're making progress, gathering more and more information before

taking the next step and really testing what you've learned. It's
good to do this early, but you need to move on quick.

◆ *Experimental—I will:* This is where you rigorously test your
best guesses and your hypothesis. You commit to running an
experiment for a period of time. In practice, the experimental
approach sounds like this: I'll test...for [duration]...to learn...

For Margot, after spending a few months running the organic and
exploratory process, she might have arrived somewhere like this:
'*I'll test* a minimum viable pilot of my online platform, offering it
for free to my email list *for* three months *to learn* via live feedback
from users about what they want and don't want'.

The Experiment Mindset is wonderfully flexible and diverse, and your
experiments don't need to be extreme or public. The size doesn't matter
but the learning does. Start small, learn fast and scale what works.

Here are some other examples so you can see how flexible this
mindset really is:

- *I'll test* walking to work twice a week *for* a month *to learn* if it
  helps me start the day calmer.
- *I'll test* saying no to one non-essential meeting each week *for*
  eight weeks *to learn* how it affects my focus.
- I'll test writing for ten minutes each morning *for* two weeks *to
  learn* if it helps me think more clearly.
- *I'll test* eating lunch away from my desk *for* a fortnight *to learn*
  if I feel more refreshed in the afternoon.
- *I'll test* leaving my phone outside the bedroom *for* a week *to
  learn* if I sleep better.
- *I'll test* scheduling one coffee catch-up a week *for* a month *to
  learn* if it builds my confidence in networking.

- *I'll test* starting each day by checking in with my team *for* two weeks *to learn* if it boosts connection.
- *I'll test* finishing work by 6 pm every night *for* ten days *to learn* what boundaries do for my energy.

The experiment scale starts at organic with no barrier to entry. It's an opportunity to look back on what's happened to inform where to start. Absolutely no danger exists in doing this. Do it, and move to the next step quickly.

Entering the exploratory phase might raise the heart rate a bit. It can be scary, and exciting, testing new things and trying them out publicly to see how they fit. Overall, though, it's about as risky as trying on a new hat. If the feedback isn't glowing, you can try a different hat.

The experimental phase is where you commit for a bit longer. This is higher risk; however, when you set the experiment up well, which you're learning to do throughout this book, any risk will be well mitigated. You won't really have any room to fail, because you're just gathering your data. This phase is more like getting a new haircut—a little riskier, but your hair will grow back.

The experimental approach follows a loop that I call the Experiment Mindset cycle. You will have already seen parts of this cycle in action, in your own life and in Margot's story, but most people skip some key bits.

When you use the Experiment Mindset deliberately, it becomes a framework for continuous growth. This is how the brain actually learns, by predicting, testing and updating.

The Experiment Mindset cycle

You may notice how closely the Experiment Mindset cycle mirrors the process of self-directed neuroplasticity I outlined in chapter 2. Remember, your brain needs awareness, focused experience, reflection and consolidation.

The Experiment Mindset cycle aligns with this, and this is why it works — because we've evolved to grow this way.

Let's look at each of the steps in the Experiment Mindset cycle more closely.

Reflection

You *start* at reflection. While this might feel a bit counterintuitive, it's an important differentiator between this method and current approaches to personal development. The starting point for those approaches is often setting a goal, without being clear about your starting point or considered about whether it's the right goal to take you where you want to go.

In the Experiment Mindset cycle, this first step of reflection might start with horizon setting (refer to chapter 3) if you want a broader life change. It might start with a journalling process to work out whether the problem you're trying to solve is actually the problem, or what the behaviour you're trying to shift is triggered by. It might start by working out which of your three levers is the one to work with first, or by gathering baseline data. I cover some practical ways to do this in the coming pages.

An important part of this stage is that you choose a deliberate aspect to test, building awareness before setting your hypothesis.

Build hypothesis

In science, a hypothesis is a testable prediction. It's a statement you can prove or disprove. With the Experiment Mindset, however, you're not really trying to 'prove' anything; you're trying to learn.

So, the behavioural version of a hypothesis becomes the approach outlined earlier in this chapter: I'll test *[action]* for *[duration]* to learn *[what you want to understand]*.

This is a statement of curiosity, not certainty. You're saying, 'Here's what I think might happen. Let's find out'.

Test

This stage is where you gain the all-important lived experience—that is, you do the thing and see what happens. Make sure you stay the course (unless it's unsafe) so that you can really gather the learnings. This process is not meant to feel easy, so don't check out too soon. The struggle is normal when you're trying something new.

Measure

At this stage, you gather the data. Remember—you're not looking for 'pass' or 'fail'; you're measuring to collect data and learn.

The data you're collecting and learning from comes in two types:

1. *External:* These are your tangible metrics—the things you can actually measure. If you're looking to reduce stress, for example, you might be looking at heart rate variability or resting heart rate on your smart watch to see how it changes in response to your intervention. If you're looking to improve your public speaking, you might survey your audience. For Margot and her personal development business for professional women, external data could be how many people signed up to her online platform. She could also look at revisit rates and which pages they used the most. She could also consider any responses to feedback forms.

2. *Internal:* This data is more connected to how you feel. It's harder to measure, but easy to record and track through a journal. The internal data you gather and how structured you are is going to depend on what you're testing. For some things, you're just going to know whether it's working for you or not.

Reflection (again)

And then, you close the loop, arriving back at reflection. You're further down the track than where you were before, and the learnings you've gathered from the measure phase allow you to decide what to do next. You can now choose to adapt, abort or anchor:

- *Adapt:* Take the learnings and adapt your approach before running your next experiment. This is how you truly evolve your thinking and yourself.
- *Anchor:* You like what you've discovered and so you double-down on it.
- *Abort:* You call it quits. The experiment taught you that you were on the wrong track, so you abort the experiment completely and decide to do something else. You still take with you the wisdom gained through the experience.

The following figure shows the full Experiment Mindset cycle.

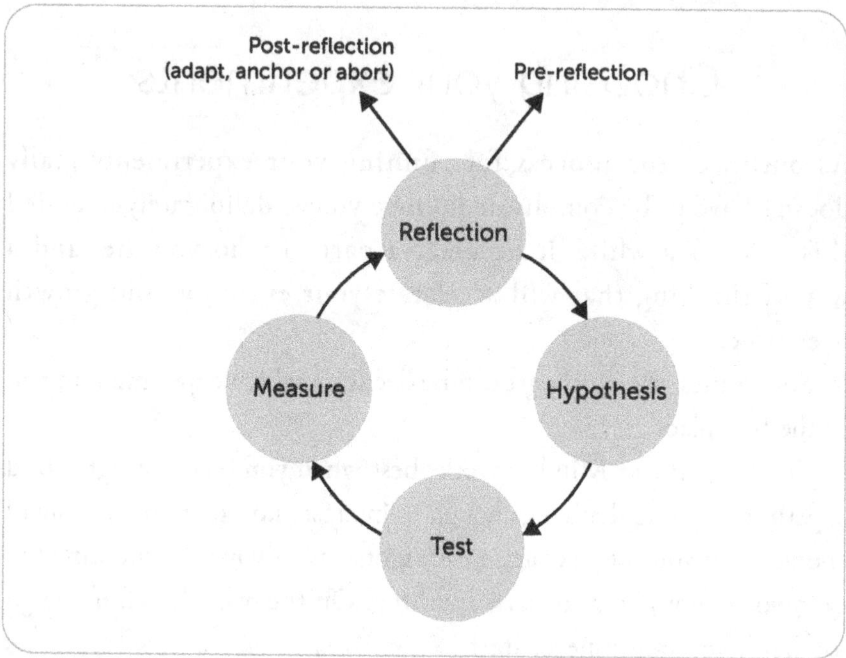

The Experiment Mindset cycle

If you've had anything to do with new product or AI launches, you may notice the approach there is similar. A minimal viable product (MVP) is decided on and then offered to the public or staff for feedback. Based on this feedback and other data gathered over the test period, the prototype is classed as a 'go', 'hold' or 'no-go'. 'Go' means the data was positive and the prototype should be developed further, 'hold' means the idea holds promise but needs more development, while 'no-go' means the data does not justify further investment. Importantly, the process is fast (and as cheap as possible) so people can quickly gather data, adjust as needed and move to the next stage—without any mention of failure. This is done in the tech world to avoid wasted time, money and energy in an area that can be very expensive, time-consuming and rapidly changing. So it makes sense to expand this concept out to the realm of personal and professional growth. This focus on data, learning and adjusting is what the Experiment Mindset is all about.

Choosing your experiments

As outlined, the process for running your experiments really doesn't have to be complicated. Once you've deliberately operated this way for a while, it becomes a part of who you are, and a way of thinking that will accelerate your evolution and growth over time.

Sometimes, the hard part can be deciding which experiment to run in the first place.

The Experiment Mindset works best when you pick the right sized experiment—one that's big enough to interest and excite you, but small enough that you can take action straightaway. If you do something too easy, you're not going to learn anything. On the other hand, if you go too hard, you might never start.

You need to strike a balance between something you can achieve at a stretch and will make a meaningful difference, and something you can maintain.

You can get there using two core frameworks.

Focusing on impact, confidence and ease

If you're anything like me, when you're staring at a list of ideas or you're feeling excited about something, your brain wants to do everything at once. When it comes to growth, though, less really is more. When you set things up well and choose the right experiments, you take smaller steps but the learnings compound over time to take you further than you ever thought possible.

The impact, confidence and ease (ICE) framework helps you decide where to start:

- *Impact:* How much of a difference is this experiment likely to make?
- *Confidence:* How sure am I that it's going to work?
- *Ease:* How hard will implementing it be?

This framework is a quick, practical prioritisation tool that I've borrowed from innovation and design science (and was originally attributed to entrepreneur Sean Ellis). You can outwardly score it if you like, or just run it through in your mind.

The experiments that are high in impact, high in confidence and high in ease are the ones you'll want to run first.

ICE example: Putting your phone away after 6 pm

For each of your potential experiments, score it from 1 to 10 on the three elements in the ICE framework to help you work out which one to focus on first. The following table outlines the questions to ask, and includes example responses for the possible experiment of putting your phone away after 6 pm.

(continued)

<table>
<tr><td colspan="3">ICE framework example: I'll test putting my phone away after 6 pm for a week to learn if my evenings feel calmer.</td></tr>
<tr><td>Impact</td><td>If this works, how much of a difference is it going to make?</td><td>I look at my phone a lot, and I really don't need to. It's distracting me from time with my family and making me feel like work never ends. Not looking at it after 6 pm could make a big difference. I'll say 7/10 impact.</td></tr>
<tr><td>Confidence</td><td>How confident am I that I can do it?</td><td>It'll require discipline, but I can do it. Nothing is that urgent. I'll say 8/10 for confidence.</td></tr>
<tr><td>Ease</td><td>How easy is it to start?</td><td>I don't need anything to start. So 9/10 for ease.</td></tr>
</table>

Add the three numbers together. The highest total usually points to your best next step—that is, the experiment that will have a meaningful impact and that you can start soon.

You don't need to overthink your ratings within the ICE framework. It's just a way to get you moving if not knowing where to start has you procrastinating. The next thing to check is whether your experiment is stretching you enough to keep it interesting, and not so much that you're stressed to the eyeballs.

Finding your Goldilocks zone for growth

You no doubt know the story of Goldilocks and her porridge. One bowl is too hot, the other too cold and the one she finally settled in to eat was just right. Your experiments work like this too.

Growth requires tension. You need enough pressure to spark change, but not so much that it breaks you.

Back in 1908, psychologists Robert Yerkes and John Dodson mapped the relationship between arousal and performance. They discovered that stress and performance actually rise together, but only up to a point. If you push it too far, performance falls away and stress takes over.

They called it the Yerkes–Dodson Law, which is really just a scientific description of what we intuitively feel. When you're stretched just enough, you feel excited, curious, energised and engaged. When you're stressed and scared, your performance dips as you flip from learning mode to survival mode.

As shown in the following figure, not enough stress has you coasting in your comfort zone, safe but not learning. The right amount of pressure sets the bar high enough to keep you excited and engaged—and in the growth zone. Too much pressure, and you're stressed, anxious and at risk of burning out and tapping out.

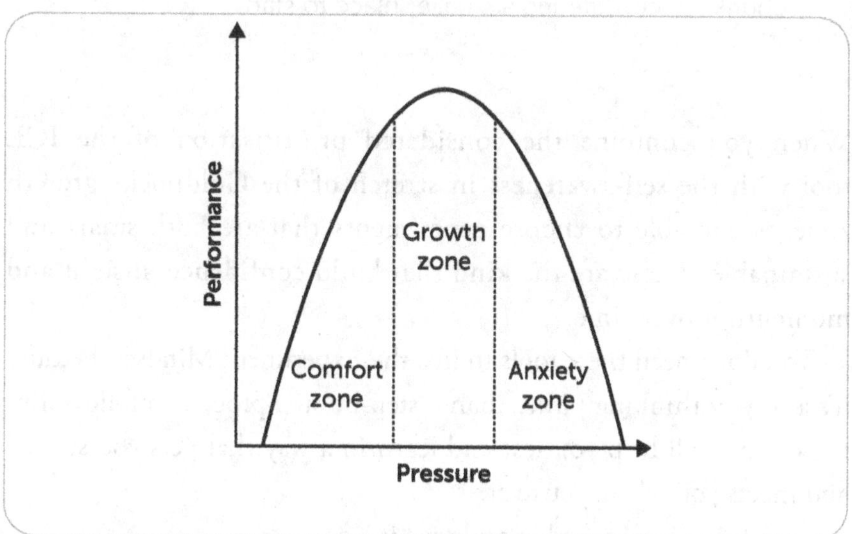

The Yerkes–Dodson Curve and the relationship between performance and pressure

As neuroscientist Andrew Huberman often puts it (including in discussions on his podcast Huberman Lab), 'The ideal learning state is alert but calm. High focus, low fear'. That's the Goldilocks zone of growth—the sweet spot where challenge fuels learning rather than blocking it.

> ### Find your Goldilocks growth zone
>
> Here's how to recognise which Goldilocks zone you're in:
>
> ◆ *Under-challenged:* You're comfortable but disengaged. Stretch yourself by adding novelty, risk or accountability. Sometimes simply adding a deadline can up the stakes enough.
> ◆ *Optimal zone:* You're alert, learning fast, and stretched but not stressed out. Aim here.
> ◆ *Over-challenged:* You're reactive, stressed or tired, and often all three. Try breaking your experiment down into smaller chunks or considering a smaller place to start.

When you combine the considered prioritisation of the ICE tool with the self-awareness in stretch of the Goldilocks growth zone, you're able to choose experiments that are both smart and sustainable. These are the kind that build confidence, insight and momentum over time.

You don't need these tools to live the Experiment Mindset, because it's a way of thinking rather than a step-by-step process to follow. But these tools will help you test and learn in a way that gets you started and meets you where you're at.

Let's bring it all together and give it a go.

Design your first experiment

It's time to stop trying to think, or read, your way to change. You don't need to get to the end of this book to start; instead, I encourage you to start now. Clarity doesn't come before action, it follows it. If you wait until you're certain, you'll never start.

Let's run the process and see where you can start.

Grab your journal or a piece of paper, and write down your responses to the following questions.

Reflection: What's actually going on?

Here's where you build awareness about your starting point. Are you repeating any patterns, or noticing any niggling feelings in your gut that you're off track? Why do you think you picked up this book in the first place?

Use these prompts to surface where you're at:

◆ What's working right now? What's giving you energy?
◆ What's draining you or keeping you stuck?
◆ If nothing changed in this area for six months, how would that feel?
◆ Which lever is the required change mainly driven by (environment, physiology, psychology)?
◆ What's one small shift that would make a meaningful difference?

People tend to skip through the pre-reflection, awareness building stage too quickly, because they're impatient and it feels slow; however, as a result, they miss the gold. Be honest with yourself and don't be afraid to ask the hard questions. No-one's watching!

(continued)

Hypothesis: Turn awareness into action

Take what you've learned and test your best first step. Remember—you're not setting a goal to 'succeed'; you're running an experiment to learn where to go next.

Use this framework: *I'll test* [action] *for* [duration] *to learn* [what I want to understand]. For example:

◆ *I'll test* finishing work by 6 pm *for* two weeks *to learn* what boundaries do for my energy and my workload.

◆ *I'll test* asking for feedback after meetings *for* a month *to learn* how others experience my leadership.

Prioritise with ICE (if you need to)

Not all experiments are created equal. Some will stretch you more, some will drain you faster, some require a heap of resources, and some require so much approval from others that they'll never get off the ground.

When you feel excited by everything or stuck by choice, use the ICE framework to decide where to start.

Rate each idea on a scale of 1 to 10 for each element of the ICE framework.

ICE element	Question	Score
Impact	If this works, how much of a difference would it make?	
Confidence	How sure am I that I can do it?	
Ease	How easy is it to start right now?	
		Total score:

Reflect on what the scores tell you about where to start.

Find your Goldilocks zone

The Goldilocks growth sweet spot, what neuroscientists call the optimal zone of arousal, is where you're alert but calm. You're focused but not freaked out.

Decide where your experiment sits right now: too easy, just right or too hard. Then reflect on what this tells you:

- If it feels too easy, how could you raise the stakes?
- If it feels too hard, how could I make it smaller or safer?

The magic of momentum lies in 'just right'. Your experiment should be not so much that you burn out, and just enough that you wake up.

Test: Do the thing

Take action, observe and stay with your experiment long enough to learn what you need to. Write down the following.

Start date: _______________________

Duration: _______________________

How I'll track my learnings: _______________________

Measure: Gather your data

The goal isn't to pass or fail but to collect evidence. Look for two kinds of data:

- *External:* Tangible results—for example, steps taken, responses, outcomes or time saved.
- *Internal:* Felt experience—for example, energy, confidence or clarity. Also note what you noticed and what surprised you.

Reflection (again)

You're back at the start and you've closed the loop. Ask yourself:

- What's clearer now than before?
- What did this teach you about yourself?
- What might you test next?

(*continued*)

Evidence to keep you moving

The sad thing about the Margot story from the start of this chapter is that she wasn't totally off track. The platform she wanted to build really could have changed lives, but it never got the chance because she became so disheartened that she stopped. It's easy to do, isn't it? We pour our energy into the outcome, convinced that if we just work hard enough, it will all click into place. But when the results don't come, it's not just the project that falls apart but also our confidence.

Our relentless focus on the end goal isn't getting us to where we want to go. But the momentum generated by small, deliberate experiments and the compounding impact they create really can. That's why I'm writing this book. The only real risk in this chapter is you feeling like you need to do these experiments perfectly. Feeling like that could break apart the very thing I'm trying to build—the simplicity of test and learn thinking. So I'm trusting you to take what you need and move.

Because when you operate this way, you start gathering real evidence. Not the kind that tells you you've 'made it', but the kind that proves you can figure things out as you go. Evidence that you're capable, adaptable and resourceful, and that even when something doesn't go to plan, you know how to learn from it.

Over time, that evidence starts to shift how you see yourself. You begin to trust your own data more than anyone else's, and you move from chasing success to building wisdom.

That's where we're heading next. Because intelligence gathers information, but wisdom knows what to do with it.

Reflection prompts

- What are you currently over-planning that you could just test instead?
- Looking at your list of things you want to change, which one would teach you the most if you tested it this week?
- Right now, are you coasting in comfort, stretched in growth or stressed beyond learning?
- If this experiment can't fail because you're just gathering data, what are you actually afraid of?

8

Translating information to wisdom

Australian business strategist Stacey Packer was sitting across from me at a cafe when she described what perimenopause felt like. 'I feel like a stranger in my own body', she said. 'Sometimes I'll be mid-sentence with a client and just … lose the word I was about to say. Gone. Or I'll wake up at 3 am with my heart racing for no reason.'

She'd spent months reading conflicting advice for dealing with the symptoms. One expert said fasting was the answer while another said fasting was dangerous for hormone health. One said cut carbs, another said add carbs. One said lift heavy weights, another said do some yoga. One said take hormone replacement therapy, another said it's an absolute last resort. 'I didn't know who to trust', she told me. 'So after chatting to you about experimentation, I decided to trust myself.'

Working with her GP, Stacey started small. First, she tested a shift in medication, which helped stabilise her mood. Then she read about intermittent fasting and decided to run a personal experiment. Her hypothesis was 'I'll test 16:8 fasting for four weeks to learn if it reduces brain fog and improves energy'.

She tracked the following in a simple journal: energy levels (1 to 10), brain fog (yes/no), mood (three words). Here's what she noted:

- *Week 1:* Energy dropped to 4/10. Brain fog worse. Mood: irritable, exhausted, shaky.
- *Week 2:* Same.
- *Week 3:* Worse.

By week four, she was done. 'I was so tired I could barely function', she said. 'I can't afford to be like that in my job.' But instead of beating herself up, she gathered her data, did more research, and found a nutrition plan specifically focused on hormones and health. Within two weeks, she felt vibrant and, within a month, the brain fog had lifted.

'The obvious win is that I made progress', she told me. 'But what struck me most was how much agency I felt. I wasn't a victim of perimenopause anymore. I was back in the driver's seat.'

That's what happens when you start experimenting. You stop fighting with yourself and start learning from yourself, becoming your own best ally rather than feeling at war. This mindset gives you back agency when life feels uncertain, not by promising control over your outcomes, but by teaching you how to learn from them.

In treating yourself like your own N-of-1 experiment, you're building your own personal wisdom.

Understanding the difference between being smart and being wise

Being smart is different from being wise. Knowledge can be collected like books. It can be accumulated over years and left on a beautiful bookshelf for a lifetime, gathering dust—giving an impression of wisdom, but never really being cracked open and used. This knowledge is really just shelves and shelves of potential, waiting to be brought to life.

The building of wisdom is one area where the greats of science, psychology and philosophy agree. As author Ryan Holiday titled his latest book, 'Wisdom takes work. Learn, apply, repeat'. Philosopher and poet Ralph Waldo Emerson expressed throughout his works the importance of action for learning. He argued without action, thought 'can never ripen into truth', and that a wise person's words 'are loaded with life'. Humanist psychologist Erik Erikson and his wife, Joan Erikson, an artist and author, studied life's stages, ageing and wisdom extensively. Joan explained in a meeting with Dan Goleman back in 1988 that wisdom 'comes from life experience, well digested. It's not what comes from reading great books. When it comes to understanding life, experiential learning is the only worthwhile kind; everything else is hearsay'.

Your 'book of wisdom' comes blank, ready to be filled through the writings and reflections of a life lived. It is filled by knowledge applied in the real world, pressure tested and scrutinised, with a lens of the unavoidable honesty of the data in front of you.

Most people never fill their book. They keep stacking knowledge on the shelf, thinking the next bit of information is the missing piece, the one that'll provide the answer you've been waiting for. It feels like progress, but the book stays blank — because filling it requires something harder than learning. It requires taking action, and then really looking at what happened, not what you hoped would happen. It requires deep and honest reflection, and reflection can hurt.

Learning from the teabag experiment

A few years ago, I was running a workshop where I demonstrated one of my favourite mind–body experiments. I get everyone in the audience to hold up a teabag on a string and I ask them to move it just by thinking about it. Usually, I can get about 90 per cent of an audience to get it happening. This sounds like magic, but it's actually neuroscience. The experiment shows how external prompts can command your brain and body to act without you even realising it. In what's called the 'ideomotor effect', you visualise the movement, and your brain sends micro-signals to your muscles that create tiny, unconscious movements. You're not willing the teabag to move through magic. You're demonstrating how thought translates to physical action before conscious awareness.

For those in my audience who don't get their teabag moving, it's usually simply because they don't believe it's possible, or they're giving their brain a conflicting command.

In this particular workshop, a man named Alex couldn't get it to happen. He sat there looking pensive, and I started to wonder if he wasn't enjoying the workshop.

A week later, I got an email. In it, Alex told me he'd been thinking about that experiment ever since. He said he didn't have a great relationship with his own mind, and he thought the teabag not moving might be reflective of that. He was willing the teabag to move, and it wouldn't. He took this as feedback that something was wrong with him, and I wondered if that belief was sitting behind the scenes as he tried to command that teabag to move. While he felt a desire for the teabag to move, he also held an opposing belief that he wasn't capable.

Alex ended up engaging me for some coaching. He explained that he felt average at a lot of things and excellent at none. On the outside, he looked successful. He was a senior leader in an agriculture business, exceeding his targets every year, impressing his bosses and making enough money to buy everything he needed. But he felt hollow inside and didn't think he was capable of finding joy anymore.

When we first sat down together, I asked, 'What do you want?'

His body language read somewhere between sad and irritated. 'I don't know. That's why I'm here.'

Beneath the response was a heaviness that was palpable in the room, and a sense that life had trained him to stop expecting anything to change. I needed to find another way to connect with him, so I started with his story. What I discovered was telling.

Alex wasn't average at everything; in fact, far from it. He'd grown multiple businesses as a general manager, taking them from barely profitable to thriving. Twice, he'd been on track for promotion, only to have the opportunity pulled away by factors outside of his control.

At one point he decided to stop building other people's visions and launched his own consultancy in the hospitality industry. It did really well, and then COVID-19 hit. His focus for the consultancy was international tourism, and that market disappeared overnight so his business collapsed, and he went back to employment.

He'd also started a successful YouTube channel, generating sponsorship opportunities, until a few followers complained about him promoting products, so he pulled back.

He'd played high-level sport but gave it up after their league changed and he had to travel for an hour each way to play and train.

Pattern after pattern. Alex would accelerate rapidly toward success, and then fall back to baseline when the feedback from the world wasn't aligning with his goals. It was like he was progressing, hitting a trampoline wall, and bouncing back to the start. He felt, and even looked, knocked around by life and, over time, he'd lost faith.

On the surface, it looked like Alex was running experiments and taking action based on the feedback from those experiments, just like I've been suggesting through the pages in this book. But his system for growth collapsed with his interpretation of the data. When things didn't go the way he wanted or expected, instead of asking, 'What can I learn from this? What experiment do I run next to keep me in momentum?', he took the data as proof he wasn't good enough and he should stop.

He wasn't failing to experiment. He was failing to learn from the experiments. Here's the pattern he was following:

- *The data:* Promotion didn't come through.
- *His interpretation:* I'm not good enough.
- *The data:* COVID-19 killed the consultancy.
- *His interpretation:* I'm not cut out to run my own thing.
- *The data:* YouTube followers complained about sponsorships.
- *His interpretation:* My audience doesn't want sponsorships; what's the point in continuing.

Every time he gathered data, he skipped the reflection phase and, instead, instinctively interpreted the data as failure and retreated. He never stayed in the experiment long enough to learn from it.

Joan Erikson, in the same meeting with Dan Goleman, observed, 'Lots of old people don't get wise, but you don't get wise unless you age'. I'd argue that if some people can grow old without growing wise, then some people who aren't yet old can still grow wise. Because it's not about the ageing at all; it's about the reflection.

Some of Alex's experiments should have ended. His decisions weren't necessarily wrong or bad. Going back to employment after COVID-19 wasn't wrong. Stepping away from a role with no growth opportunity wasn't wrong. Choosing to avoid crazy travel and wasted hours in his week for sport wasn't wrong.

But he wasn't ending experiments because he'd learned what he needed to know. He was ending them because the data felt like rejection and it hurt, reinforcing the belief that he was Captain Average. This belief then leaked through every area of his life.

When a scientist runs an experiment, they're not looking to validate their ideas or to win. Their goal is the data. They're looking for information. What's working? What's not? What's surprising? What else could be true? Alex was instead looking for validation, and when he didn't get it, he stopped. This is protection rather than learning, and defence over curiosity.

When we worked together, we didn't focus on running new experiments straightaway. We focused on going back through the ones he'd already run. Similar to what I outlined in chapter 6 when looking at the psychology lever, we ran retrospective belief experiments, gathering different data on events that had already passed. Alex was learning whether the beliefs that he had reinforced through the events of his life were simply *a* truth, rather than *the* truth.

What actually happened when the promotion didn't come through? External restructure. It wasn't based on his performance.

What actually happened with the consultancy? A global pandemic shut down international tourism. His business model was working until an unforeseeable event made the entire market disappear.

What actually happened with YouTube? A small percentage of followers complained. The majority didn't. And plenty of successful creators monetise their content.

The data hadn't changed. His interpretation did.

Most beliefs aren't truths; they're hypotheses. This means they can be tested. Through looking at old data from a different direction, forming a new hypothesis and taking it out for testing, you're able to gain new knowledge and understanding. When this is done repeatedly over time, you gather wisdom.

Once Alex saw his experiences from a different angle, possibility opened up for him again. He had hope. He could see what to do next.

He didn't need to start over; he just needed to adjust.

Alex got back on YouTube and started creating again. He learned how to integrate product promotions more organically into his content, and he experimented with new ways of doing things. Did he stop getting the odd piece of feedback about promoting products? No. Did his channel keep growing? Yes. It grew exponentially the more consistently he posted, and people learned over time what type of content to expect from him. He just needed to stay in the game long enough to get the real data.

He watched his data with curiosity rather than judgement, and interpreted it in a way that allowed him to evolve rather than stop. He turned his data into wisdom.

This is a skill to be learned, and that's what this chapter is about.

Introducing the Wisdom Cycle

Back in chapter 3, I talked briefly about the idea that information alone isn't enough. It's what you do with it that counts. Here, we're going to slow down and turn that into a practical model you can actually use.

Alistair Horscroft, one of my most influential teachers and mentors, first introduced me to Russell Ackoff's DIKW (Data–Information–Knowledge–Wisdom) pyramid (also known as the 'data pyramid' or 'knowledge pyramid'). While the terms and depiction of the elements have evolved over the years, Horscroft explained to me that information applied to baseline data leads to new data, which leads to increased knowledge. Over time, you reach the pinnacle: wisdom.

I've adapted the model as I've come to see it less as a pyramid and more as a cycle, containing the crucial element of reflection. I call this the Wisdom Cycle (shown in the following figure).

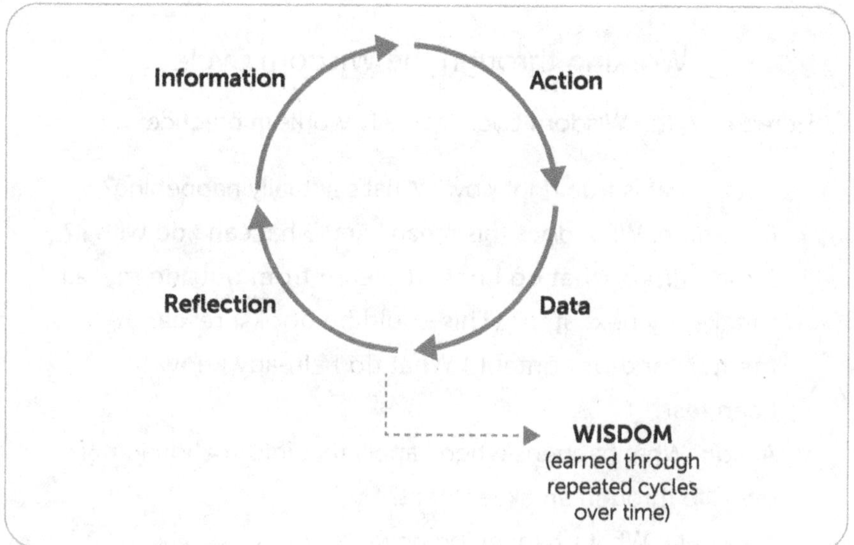

The Wisdom Cycle

The cycle always starts with reflecting on your data—these are your raw observations, and the qualitative and quantitative feedback from your life. It takes courage to take a good hard look at your starting point, especially when it's not where you want it to be. If you're unhappy in your body, your relationships, your job or your life, the easy thing to do is look outward to gather more information and set goals about what you want instead. The hard thing to do is to stare down your starting point and analyse it to find where the real gap is between what you have and what you want. But that's where the magic happens. The growth sits in the discomfort.

As mentioned, most people skip this stage. They jump straight into the mindless consumption of more information, thinking that's what will get them ahead. They focus on another podcast, another book or another course. It feels productive, but it's not. It's high-quality procrastination.

Working through the Wisdom Cycle

Here's how the Wisdom Cycle actually works in practice:

◆ *Data:* What is true right now? What's actually happening?
◆ *Reflection:* What does this mean? And what can I do with it?
◆ *Information:* What do I need to learn from outside myself to take my next step? (This could be books, research, mentors and/or content.) What do I already know that I can test?
◆ *Action:* What happens when I apply that information in my own life through an experiment?
◆ *New data:* What's happening now?
◆ *Repeat.*

This maps directly onto the experiment cycle outlined in the last chapter:

◆ Data is what you measure.
◆ Reflection is where you turn that data into awareness.
◆ Information helps you form your hypothesis.
◆ Action is when you test.

This cycle of learning, testing and reflection is how experimentation works. It's also how the accumulation of wisdom works, how neuroplasticity works and how growth works. That's why it echoes all throughout this book.

Information is great to have; it makes you smarter and increases the number and quality of your potential decisions. But information alone won't change your life. When you stay in the cycle, when you complete each loop, you don't just gather more information but start to see patterns. You learn what works for you, not just what works in theory. You build a personal library of evidence you can actually trust.

That's wisdom.

Gathering data: Track what you're testing

In chapter 7, I ran through how to design your experiment and set your hypothesis: *I'll test* [action] *for* [duration] *to learn* [what I want to understand]. To gather your data, you now need to actually track whether it's working.

I'm not going to prescribe the practicalities of how you track your data, because you need to find what works best for you. Run an N-of-1 on it.

You might track data through:

- the notes section of your phone
- a physical journal
- an app
- etches in stone.

I really don't mind, as long as it's something you'll actually do. If you're considering spending hours making a fancy spreadsheet and never taking action on it, please head back to the start of the book.

The mistake I often see people making at this stage is that they either track nothing and rely on fuzzy feelings, or they track everything and drown in data they don't know what to do with. The solution is to simply track what you're testing. For example:

- If you're testing whether walking to work twice a week helps you start the day calmer, track your walking and how calm you feel.

- If you're testing whether saying no to commitments gives you more energy, track your ratio of saying yes to no, and your energy.
- If you're testing whether asking for feedback helps you grow as a leader, track the feedback and how it changes your behaviour.

You're looking for two types of data.

- *External data:* This is the measurable stuff. What exactly happened? How many times? What was the outcome?
- *Internal data:* This is the felt experience. How did it feel? What did you notice? What surprised you?

Both matter. You need external data to know what actually happened, and you need internal data to know what it means.

We can use Alex's example to see what that looks like in practice.

Alex's YouTube experiment

When Alex returned to his YouTube channel, we treated it as a three-month experiment. His hypothesis was '*I'll test* posting consistently *for* three months *to learn* whether consistency improves growth'.

Before this, Alex had been watching his metrics, but he was putting too much weight on a couple of critical comments. That wasn't high-quality data, and we knew it wasn't supportive of his growth because he stopped. Alex's Wisdom Cycle had morphed into information, action, data, very brief reflection, too uncomfortable — *abort*.

This time was different because he was clearer on the experiment and he tracked only what mattered.

His external data was as follows:

- whether or not he included product promotions
- views

- impressions
- click-through rate
- average view duration
- subscribers (growth over time)
- affiliate conversions.

His internal data came through noting how he felt posting each video, and whether this was resistance or ease.

The shift was immediate — not in results, but in clarity and confidence.

Month 1

In the first month, views were lower than they used to be, because he'd taken a break and needed to rebuild. The other external data was a bit all over the place. For his internal data, he wrote notes with words like 'felt exposed', 'rusty' and 'vulnerable', but he kept going because his job was to notice this data, not to judge it.

Month 2

By the second month, things started to look a bit more like he was used to, and affiliate conversions started to appear. He felt more grounded and he was re-engaging with his craft, getting more creative and excited about it again. He felt some momentum building.

Month 3

This was the month everything started to compound, with views climbing sharply, watch time growing, and people commenting and engaging. The algorithm picked up his consistency and rewarded it.

But the bigger shift was internal, because Alex felt steadier and more confident. Everything wasn't perfect and he did have some comments about product promotions, but because he'd been tracking things over time he finally understood why things were moving.

He could see that consistency did, in fact, lead to growth. He then started to have fun, playing around with different variables and seeing how the data changed as a result. He'd stopped treating every comment, every metric and every wobble as a verdict, and started looking at the data like a scientist, not a critic.

The data was there before, but he'd related to it differently, causing him to fail in the only way an experiment can fail—by stopping too early, and by not learning and iterating.

A few comments weren't derailing him anymore, because he was looking for patterns rather than occasional blips. If comments did become consistent enough to take notice, he treated them as data and adapted. He'd learned to trust the signal, rather than the noise.

But knowing what feedback to take and what feedback to leave is difficult. We've all been in a position where we've had to stomach feedback we didn't ask for. So how do we navigate that without derailing?

Delving into feedback

When your experiment involves leading a team, starting a business, presenting an idea or putting your work out into the world, feedback becomes unavoidable. How you handle it determines whether you learn from it or let it derail you.

In my own journey to dealing productively with feedback, I'll never forget my first big keynote.

A mentor and friend of mine, someone about five years ahead of me in his speaking career, had been offered the opportunity to speak at New Zealand's Flight Centre team conference, which that year was being held in Adelaide. He couldn't make it, so he recommended me.

This was seven years ago, and up until that point the largest audience I'd spoken to was 50 people. Suddenly I was standing in front of an international audience of 350, a room full of people who were used to world-class speakers and cutting-edge content.

I prepared relentlessly, and it paid off. From my perspective it went well, and I was genuinely proud of myself for being brave enough to stand up there (and I still am). The conference organiser's immediate feedback was glowing.

Then, about a week later, a feedback email landed in my inbox, with a line of feedback from every single audience member—all 350 of them. Even now, after nine years of professional speaking, this is the only time this has happened.

Although the detail took me by surprise, when you put your work into the world, whether it's speaking, writing or creating content, you learn pretty quickly that you can't be for everyone. If you try to be, you end up safe and a little boring. So, yes, some negative feedback is inevitable, but that doesn't make it easy.

Back to the email, and from the top, things were looking great:

- 'Wish we had her for longer.'
- 'Highlight of the conference.'
- 'Someone every leader should listen to.'

Over 300 positive pieces of feedback, but do you think those are the ones my brain held on to? Of course not. My brain, like every human brain, went straight to these:

- 'I'd prefer someone with a more inspiring story.'
- 'I've heard all this before.'
- 'Could have had another coffee break.'

Ouch. That's the thing about feedback, however. It can be incredibly valuable and an absolute stinger. In that moment, those three comments eclipsed the other 347. They hit me like a punch in the gut, and for a moment I thought, *I never want to do that again.*

Now I think, *Imagine if I'd stopped there!* Imagine if I'd taken those three lines from three strangers and used them as evidence I wasn't good enough. Imagine if I'd let that be the end of my speaking career. This book wouldn't exist.

This is why learning how to interpret feedback matters. Remember:

- Not all feedback is created equal.
- Not all feedback is useful.
- Not all feedback is yours to take on.

The skill is learning to distinguish between the types of feedback, and knowing what to absorb and what to let bounce straight off.

Here's how you do that.

Processing feedback without letting it derail you

Neuroscientist and psychologist Lisa Feldman Barrett's research shows that your brain predicts how feedback will feel before you even receive it. If you expect threat, your brain constructs a threat response. As highlighted by research presented back in chapter 1, criticism and judgement from others activates the same neural pathways as physical pain. Your brain doesn't distinguish between 'Could have had another coffee break' and 'You're in grave danger. Run'.

While human beings do want to learn and grow, we also want to be accepted as we are right now. That's what makes feedback tricky. In their book *Thanks for the Feedback*, Harvard researchers Sheila Heen and Douglas Stone highlighted the three triggers that make feedback hard to receive:

- *Truth triggers:* The feedback feels wrong to you, unfair or unhelpful.

- *Relationship triggers:* You respond to how you feel about the person giving you the feedback and/or your relationship to them.
- *Identity triggers:* This hits at your sense of who you are, and challenges it. It pokes at your self-doubt. When your identity feels threatened, you're going to want to protect rather than learn.

Understanding which of these (or perhaps which combination) is triggering you to react in a defensive or avoidant way can help you to work through it more easily.

Exercise: Moving from feedback to wisdom

Here's the process I use—and the one I teach leaders, founders and creators—to stay in the Wisdom Cycle. It helps you take what's important from the feedback received and leave the rest.

Step 1: Expect information, not judgement

If you know feedback is coming, prime your brain before it even arrives. If you go in worried about what people think, your nervous system reacts before a single word is spoken.

If you go in with curiosity instead, seeing the feedback process as valuable and thinking, *This is information I can use or information I can leave*, you stay in a state where learning is possible.

Step 2: Pause

When feedback lands hard, don't process it immediately. Give yourself some time so you can get yourself into a reflective state rather than a protective one.

(continued)

Step 3: Identify the trigger

Once you've settled, work out which of the following might be triggering you:

- *Truth trigger:* Does this feel wrong? If it's a truth trigger, ask yourself, 'Is that defensiveness or accuracy talking?' If you're not sure, gather some more feedback or ask some deeper questions.
- *Relationship trigger:* Ask yourself, 'Do I trust this source?' If the feedback is from someone you don't trust, have a shaky relationship with or who doesn't really understand your space, consider whether that makes the feedback meaningless or biased. If you need to, run the feedback past someone you can trust.
- *Identity trigger:* If it's an identity threat, ask yourself, 'Does this hit my current identity or the one I'm growing into?' If you're doing something that's stretching your identity, remember that self-doubt is normal, as is the reality that you could have some capability gaps to grow into.

For me, the feedback from the Flight Centre conference was an identity threat. Those three comments made me question if I belonged on that stage. Thankfully, rather than deciding to abort the experiment, I chose to evolve through it, but it could have easily gone the other way.

Step 4: Look for patterns, not outliers

One person's opinion is a data point; multiple people saying the same thing is a pattern.

Out of 350 people, three didn't love my keynote—fewer than 1 per cent. And the data wasn't consistent because their critiques weren't even aligned; they weren't saying the same thing. Rather than being a pattern with a signal worth listening to, this feedback was just noise.

If 30 people had said, 'The content felt generic', that would have resulted in a different reflection.

Step 5: Find the 2 per cent truth

Even feedback you want to dismiss often contains something useful. Heen and Stone call this the '2 per cent truth'. If I go back to 'I've heard all this before', for example, and ask myself, 'Is there 2 per cent truth here?', the answer is, 'Possibly'. Back then I was early on in my career and much of my work was frameworks and tools from other people that I'd pulled together in a particular way to get my message across. That's not wrong; plenty of people work this way and it's fine as long as the original source is acknowledged. We're all standing on the shoulders of giants. But it could absolutely mean someone had seen some of it before. Now that I've created my own work and frameworks, built over time in cycles of learning and testing, it's unlikely I'll see that feedback again. But it took time to get to this point, and I couldn't start there.

It's okay to just note something down from reflecting on the feedback, without judging and berating yourself.

Step 6: Decide

With every piece of feedback, you have three options:

1. *Integrate it:* It's useful, aligned and actionable.
2. *Note it:* It might be useful later, but it's not relevant now.
3. *Dismiss it:* It's projection, preference or simply not your data.
    Let it go.

Feedback is just information, not a verdict. But make sure you're deciding what to do with it based on how useful it is, and not how it makes you feel.

Remembering who you're asking matters

Not all feedback deserves the same weight. In chapter 4, I discussed the three types of people in your environment: expanders, sustainers and drainers. When it comes to gathering feedback on your experiments, distinguishing between these types again matters. Here's why:

- Expanders are the ones ahead of you. They've done what you're trying to do or they're solving problems you're just starting to encounter. Their feedback is grounded in experience and it stretches you.
- Sustainers are your peers and allies. They keep you grounded, remind you of your strengths and help you stay steady when things wobble.
- Drainers pull you back toward who you've been. They mean well, but their feedback often sounds like, 'Are you sure?' or 'I would never do what you're doing'. They're protecting the version of you they're comfortable with.

When you're designing experiments, you need feedback from expanders. When you're navigating failure, you need support from sustainers. And when you're interpreting data, you need to recognise when a drainer is speaking so you don't let their fear become your ceiling.

Alex didn't just struggle with feedback because it hurt; he also struggled because he was taking all of it equally seriously. A few random YouTube comments carried far too much weight. He was listening to the noise, not the signal.

Curate your feedback sources the way you curate your environment—not everyone gets a vote.

It's only failure if you stop

Experimentation, neuroplastic change, wisdom and growth are all possible if you keep your Wisdom Cycle going. That doesn't mean you need to keep forcing something to work if it's not, because that's not evolution; it's the sunk-cost fallacy. Remember that progress does not equal growth. Sometimes momentum toward your horizon is a backwards or side step. And that's okay if that's what your data is telling you. It's not failure.

The only way to fail is to stop.

In the next chapter, I cover the realities of managing the process when it feels like your experiment has failed. I delve into your brain's basic instincts when it comes to failure and self-protection, and how to work around these instincts so that you can continue on and show yourself what you're really capable of.

Reflection prompts

- How many books, courses or podcasts have you consumed in the past year compared to how many experiments you've actually run?
- Do you tend more toward tracking nothing and relying on fuzzy feelings, or tracking everything and drowning in data you don't know what to do with?
- Think of some recent critical feedback. Which trigger hit hardest—truth (feels wrong), relationship (who said it) or identity (challenges who you think you are)?
- What experiment did you abandon that might have been valuable if you'd stayed in it long enough to gather real data?

9

When experiments 'fail'

My social feeds are full of inspiring memes telling me to embrace failure. Business gurus such as *The Diary of a CEO*'s Steven Bartlett encourage us to 'outfail the competition'. Organisational psychologist Adam Grant in his book *Hidden Potential* says, 'If you're not failing, you're not experimenting enough'. On paper, of course, I agree with it all. But when I'm in the thick of it, when my gut is churning, my brain is catastrophising, and I want to crawl into a hole and hide, reading this advice makes me want to throw my phone across the room. It's easy to oversimplify this tension. Let me give you some of my own examples.

My 'failed' experiments

It's all good to talk about failure in hindsight; it's much harder to live it in real time. Failure is an important part of learning and an inevitable part of experimentation, but it can feel really bloody hard.

Two failed experiments stand out in my life, leaving a lingering sting of regret. While they're very different from each other, they have one thing in common. Instead of taking the learnings and adapting, I stopped.

The *How She Does It* experiment

Back in chapter 2, I shared the moment on my New Zealand honeymoon when I realised the door to a meaningful, aligned and exciting career hadn't actually closed. I realised starting a blog might scratch the itch I had to learn and write on health and wellbeing. It was the first spark that maybe I could have work that felt aligned with how I wanted to show up in the world.

During my maternity leave with our first little boy, I took my first step. I created a blog called *How She Does It*. I wrote about navigating the shift out of the professional world to have a child, and the messy, imperfect process of stepping back in again. I interviewed other professional mums about how they made it all work. Every week I posted a meal planner with recipes and a shopping list that people could download by subscribing to my newsletter.

This was 2016, when social media still had organic reach, podcasts weren't everywhere and working-parent resources were limited. The opportunity was right there.

But I talked myself out of it. I told myself the space was saturated. I worried what people would think. Running through my head were thoughts like, *Who am I to do this? I'm not qualified. Is this lame?*

I wasn't used to putting myself out there. I was still working in medical imaging, and flying comfortably under the radar. While dabbling felt safe, changing didn't.

The bigger my blog got, the smaller I felt. Eventually, the fear won and I quit. It wasn't the first time.

The triathlon experiment

Around 15 years ago, I decided to train for a triathlon. I approached this how I often do things: make a decision and become obsessed with it. At the time, I wasn't a fast runner but I at least knew how to run.

I had never cycled, and I could swim well enough to keep myself afloat, but that's where it ended. For about six months I trained harder than I ever had. I was up at 5 am, running to the pool to swim before work, and often training twice per day to fit it all in. At the end of the day, I'd go to bed with a triathlon magazine to learn everything I could—the most efficient swimming technique, the best way to transition from the bike to the run, what food I needed to eat to fuel my body.

The day finally arrived and I felt as prepared as I could be. The triathlon was an afternoon event, which was a shift from my usual morning routine. It was also mid-February, the height of an Australian summer, and the temperature was 38 degrees Celsius. Blisteringly hot.

Surrounded by hundreds of other nervous participants, I placed my bike out and laid my gear in order, just as I'd practised. Then, brimming with nerves and excitement, we lined up at the river ready to race. Even with all of my preparation, I wasn't ready for what came next. In contrast to the heat of the air, the temperature of the water was freezing cold. It turns out that entering cold water suddenly like this, without doing a little warm-up swim first, triggers a 'cold shock' response, causing you to involuntarily gasp and hyperventilate. Your heart rate and blood pressure shoot up, causing panic and a loss of control of your breathing. On top of this, anyone who has done a triathlon will know the chaos of a swim start. In true rookie style, I didn't know to start toward the back. I was front and centre, which meant I was getting kicked, swum over and pushed around. I didn't have the space to catch my breath. It was scary.

I stopped and pulled my head above the water once the crowd started to thin out, utterly panicked. And from that moment I was unable to put my head back under without triggering the panic. I doggy paddled the entire swim leg of the triathlon, with the safety boat alongside me constantly asking me if I wanted to quit. I was too proud and too stubborn, and managed to climb out of the water dead last. Humbling doesn't even cover it.

I followed the plan and did the prep, and I absolutely tanked on the execution. The worst part of it was that because I was so embarrassed and annoyed with myself, I never tried again.

I look back on that, knowing what I know now, and kick myself. I was so fit, and I was ready to show myself what I could do. Rather than taking the really solid learnings about swim starts and trying again, however, I quit. I took what was really just a data point, and turned it into a full stop.

And that's the only way you truly fail at an experiment: you stop learning.

These two experiments stand out not because they were my biggest failures — far from it — but because they're the ones where I abandoned the process. I didn't reflect and I didn't iterate. Instead, I pulled the pin the moment things felt too confronting.

That instinct to retreat instead of learn is what this chapter is really about.

The failure reflex

One of the challenges when things go wrong is that curiosity is rarely our first instinct — defence is.

As mentioned, your brain's primary job isn't learning but protection. And failure doesn't just feel unsafe. If it involves embarrassment, exclusion or rejection, which it often does, your brain can interpret it as a genuine physical threat.

If you've ever posted something on LinkedIn that tanked, been rejected for a job or received bad feedback after a talk, you'll know that the pain doesn't just feel emotional but also physical. It can feel like a punch in the stomach or a gripping ache in the centre of your chest. That isn't just a metaphor. Neuroscience shows that social rejection can literally hurt.

Failure and the brain: Failure hurts

In 2003, researchers Naomi Eisenberger, Matthew Lieberman and Kip Williams ran an experiment to test whether social pain really does register like physical pain in the brain. They placed participants in a functional MRI scanner and asked them to play a simple virtual ball game called CyberBall. They were told two other players were playing with them in other scanners, but in reality they were simply characters in the game. Halfway through, the other two players stopped throwing the participants the ball. They were excluded (and perhaps transported back in time to high school PE class).

After the game, participants were asked to rate themselves on a distress scale. They reported feeling genuine distress — and the brain scans supported what they felt. The dorsal anterior cingulate cortex is an area of the brain that works like an alarm system, lighting up when a physical threat is detected, saying 'Hey! Pay attention, you might be in strife here!' That same alarm system fired up when these CyberBall players were left out. And the more excluded they felt, the stronger the activation.

The researchers concluded that the brain doesn't clearly distinguish between physical and social pain. We've evolved to experience social exclusion as a survival threat because, for most of human history, being pushed out of the tribe left you vulnerable and could get you killed. The brain's alarm system learned to treat rejection the same way it treats injury — as something dangerous that needs immediate attention.

This alarm system in your brain is why even small failures can feel gutting. The pain of falling short, or being criticised or left out doesn't just bruise the ego; it activates the same neural circuitry as a physical wound. The brain's job is to keep you safe, so when it registers that kind of threat, your stress response fires. Your heart rate rises, cortisol floods your system and your body gets ready to defend itself.

From there, one of three things usually happens:

- *Catastrophise:* 'I'm not cut out for this.'
- *Rationalise:* 'It wasn't that important anyway.'
- *Avoid:* 'I'm never doing this again.'

Each of these responses protects your ego in the moment, but they also rob you of learning. That's the 'failure reflex': the instinct to protect your identity instead of evolving it. But if you want to grow, your identity doesn't need protecting; it needs updating.

Updating your failure reflex

When something doesn't go to plan, any number of factors could be at play—for example:

- External circumstances you couldn't control may have had an influence.
- A capability gap may exist, meaning you just can't do it yet.
- An information gap may be present—something you didn't know before you tried.
- Maybe someone else was simply ahead of you.

Whatever the factor is, you didn't have that data before. Now you do. If you can stay regulated long enough to notice that, a fourth option becomes available: grow. You gather the data, adapt and move on to your next experiment.

Productive failure

Learning scientist Manu Kapur calls this ability to learn from setbacks 'productive failure'. His research shows that when people are allowed to struggle before being shown the right solution, they understand and retain far more. The struggle makes the learning stick. In other words, short-term discomfort leads to long-term gain—to growth.

Mistakes are effort leaving a record, marking the edge of what you know. It's important to recognise that the difference between failure and productive failure isn't the outcome; it's reflection. Without reflection, all you have is pain. With reflection, you have perspective.

Failure without reflection is trauma. Failure with reflection is growth.

The experiment post-mortem

When an experiment doesn't work, your instinct is likely to move on quickly. But that's when learning slips through your fingers. Reflection is what turns a failed outcome into useful data.

The following table outlines a simple experiment post-mortem I use with leaders and teams, and in my own life.

The experiment post-mortem

	What happened? Capture the event or outcome.	Why did it happen? Surface the causes, assumptions, emotions or system factors.	What did it teach me? Extract the insight.	How will I adjust? Turn the learning into action — iterate.
Example one: Attempting a triathlon	*I got stressed and panicked in the swim leg, and ended up doggy paddling the entire way, finishing dead last.*	*I didn't warm up for the swim and I started front and centre, when I should have been toward the back and the side to give myself more space.*	*Jumping straight into cold water causes a stress reaction, and triathlon swim starts are chaotic.*	*Warm up for the swim and start toward the back. Practise open water swimming more.*
Example two: Taking on a stretch project	*I took on a project that I'd never done before and I missed an important deadline.*	*I avoided asking for help because I didn't want to seem incapable.*	*Avoidance costs more than asking for help.*	*Flag potential blockers early and ask for input within the first week.*

This post-mortem process shifts the experience from the emotional centre of your brain to the reasoning centre. That shift lowers the threat response and makes space for curiosity. The last step in the process, 'How will I adjust?', is what keeps you moving, giving you a sense of agency and momentum.

When failure is relational and personal

Analysing a failed swim leg or a missed deadline stings, but it's containable. It's different when failure nudges against identity, trust or the people you care about. That feels personal. Reflection gives you clarity, but applying that clarity in moments that feel exposing is really hard.

These human, relational experiments can trigger your instinct to retreat more than any other kind because the cost of getting it wrong feels higher. The story you tell yourself about what the failure means can become louder than the data it gives you.

While emotional failure, relational failure and lost confidence can look different on the surface, underneath they share the same mechanism. It's the brain protecting the self instead of updating itself.

This same thing shows up at work in leaders and teams too, and sometimes the stakes and emotional complexity is even higher.

James Galdes is an Australian technology engineer, and long-term leadership coaching client. As a tech engineer early in his career, James needed to learn to overcome his tendency toward perfectionism. He learnt through mentors and experience that when it came to delivering tech solutions, over-engineering and trying to get things perfect before shipping is a waste of time if the market doesn't respond to your product in the way you think it will. You're better off creating a minimum viable solution, gathering feedback and iterating. And he became very good at that.

You'd think, then, that when it came to learning the skill of leadership, this would translate—that you could take failure as data points, iterate and grow. But James says that in leadership, like with any relationships where it feels personal and not technical, failure is much harder—because it's emotional.

On interviewing him for this book, James shared, 'When I feel I've let someone down, I don't deal with it well. That's been my biggest challenge—learning to be kind to myself, to accept I won't always get it right, and to see missteps as data, not identity'. James told me,

> *I've been in teams and built teams where the dynamics weren't right. At first, I saw that as failure. Now I see it as information. What worked? What didn't? What will I do differently next time?*
>
> *One thing I've had to learn is to be less reactive. Instead of responding immediately, I gather data and reflect, sometimes for days, before acting. In engineering, experiments are logical. In leadership, they're emotional.*

James's story captures an important point. Technical experiments are clean, while human ones are messy. They involve emotion, ego and uncertainty. What matters in these experiments isn't avoiding discomfort; it's staying in the game long enough to learn from it. (You'll hear from James again in chapter 11, when we explore how experimentation can become embedded in workplace culture.)

With human experiments, when more than one person is impacted by a failed experiment, repair becomes as important as recovery.

Research by Dr John Gottman of the Gottman Institute shows that it's not the absence of conflict in a relationship that makes success more likely but the ability to repair it. In this way, growth in relationships mirrors growth in an individual. Testing, failing, learning and reflecting together is a tool for growth, rather than something to be avoided.

Even when the intent was positive, failure in relationships only becomes real failure if you stop trying. But even when no-one else is hurt, your ego can still take a hit, and that's where confidence starts to wobble.

The confidence paradox

Paula was an emerging banking leader who joined one of my leadership programs with a clear goal. She wanted to build her confidence enough to one day step into an executive role, which was her next career step. I worked through the usual process with her to prepare her for her next role, getting her clear on her unique leadership identity, understanding her strengths and capability gaps, and making a plan to develop them. Her confidence grew enough that she was offered the role within six months and accepted it.

Then the reality hit. She had confidence enough to accept the role, but once she was in it, she realised she'd never done it before and she found it really tough. She was consistently coming up against challenges she'd never faced, and she was in rooms where she was often the only female and at least a decade younger than the people sitting alongside her. I coached her one on one through that first year as she came up against challenges, tried new ways of operating and approached tricky conversations—as she failed, repaired and adapted.

As that first year came and went, her confidence grew, and not because of any clever framework I'd given her. It grew because the best way to become the type of person who can be a banking executive is to be one. No amount of prep work will replace the act of doing the thing. Having the support and frameworks helped her stay in the game long enough to learn.

That understanding isn't new. We often tend to think confidence arrives after success, like it's something you earn once you've proven yourself worthy. But it's not as simple as that. Confidence has less to do with getting things right, and more to do with knowing that when things go wrong, you'll be able to find your footing again. That's what Paula learnt the most about herself. Even though there was a lot she didn't know yet, she learnt she could pick herself back up when she didn't get it right. What she was really building wasn't only competence but self-efficacy — the belief that she could recover from the moments she got it wrong. That's the psychological antidote to the failure reflex.

Confidence comes in the learnt belief that even if you misread the moment, misjudge the leap or completely misfire the experiment, you'll still know how to move, learn and adapt.

This is what Stanford psychologist Albert Bandura called 'self-efficacy'. It's not the belief that you'll always succeed, but the belief that you can handle what comes your way. And, crucially, self-efficacy isn't built through perfection. It's strengthened every time you fall short, stay with the discomfort, and try again.

The most successful and resilient of us have just done more reps. They've practised navigating uncertainty, stomaching setbacks and adjusting without letting the experience collapse their identity. Their confidence isn't based on the outcome; it's based on their evidence.

With this understanding, confidence stops being something fragile that rises and falls with results, and starts becoming something sturdier. It becomes a deep trust in your ability to navigate uncertainty.

Reflection prompts

◆ What experiment did you abandon when it got uncomfortable? Write down the moment you stepped away. What triggered the doubt?

◆ What data did you actually gather before you stopped? List anything you learned—even the messy or unexpected parts.

◆ What story did you tell yourself about why it was 'better' to quit? Be honest. Was it fear? Fatigue? Perfectionism? Protection?

◆ If you revisited this experiment now, what would you do differently? Think smaller, safer or more achievable steps.

◆ What's the first tiny step that would reopen this experiment? That's your next move.

Failure and the Experiment Mindset method

When you zoom out across your life, looking at the moments you quit too early, the ones you pushed through and the ones that stung but taught you something, you'll notice something. You've been gathering data on yourself all along, and every scrap of that data is useful.

Even the blog and triathlon fail taught me plenty. They gave me fodder for this book, firstly, and fuel to not repeat the same mistake again. Failure isn't final unless you stop in the face of it. Reflecting on it turns pain into information. Action on that information turns it into wisdom. And repeating the process transforms your response to failure into self-efficacy, the kind of confidence that lasts.

Failure is like a muscle: when you practise doing it well, you're training yourself to handle it better next time. The more failures you collect, the more likely success becomes.

The mechanics, science and frameworks outlined through this book don't form the heart of the Experiment Mindset. What does is the identity shift that comes from learning, again and again, that you can handle the gap between what you intended to happen and what actually happened.

Confidence, like growth and like success, isn't a finish line. It's a living system shaped by every choice you test, every limit you meet and every adjustment you make.

Failure isn't final; it's simply a data-gathering exercise.

You now have the science, the tools and the method. But knowing how to grow is very different from growing while life is still happening around you. It's one thing to design an experiment on paper; it's another to run it when the stakes are real, the outcomes are uncertain and the world keeps moving beneath your feet.

That's where the Experiment Mindset becomes more than a method and becomes a way of living.

The chapters in part IV are about taking this system into the real world—into your risks, your relationships, your work and your future. They're about taking this system into the places where growth feels uncomfortable, costly or unclear. This is where the method meets your life.

Reflection prompt

◆ What experiment in your life have you abandoned, not because it failed but because the discomfort made you doubt yourself? What would trying again actually look like now?

PART IV
Living an experimental life

As you've worked through the previous parts of this book, you've learned the science and the system behind the Experiment Mindset. But the real challenge isn't designing experiments. It's living them.

Life doesn't pause just because you've decided to grow. Circumstances shift, pressures pile on, people disappoint you and the world hands you feedback you didn't ask for. Not everyone has a safety net. And out in the real world is where your relationship with experimentation is truly tested, where things are messy and unpredictable, and rarely go according to plan.

Getting knocked around by the weight of it all is easy. But you have a thousand ways to respond when life moves beneath your feet, and the very last one is to give up on your own potential. Because living an experimental life isn't about being fearless, but being wise enough to work with what's real. It's about staying open when the world contracts, and keeping on learning, even when the outcome isn't what you expect. That's what this part of the book is about.

In the following chapters, I outline how to find, create and curate the environments where the Experiment Mindset can thrive, in your work, your relationships and your life. I show you how to experiment safely, minimising risk without losing momentum, how to build cultures that support growth and, ultimately, how to live this mindset as an ongoing practice.

Before you can build cultures where experimentation is normal, you need to learn how to make it safe for ourselves, and how to take risks without breaking the things that matter.

That's where we'll begin this part.

10

Minimising risk without losing momentum

I was partway through writing this book when I was invited to host a mental health panel for Flinders University. On that panel was Taimi Allan, South Australia's Mental Health Commissioner, Deputy Chair of the e-Mental Health International Collaborative, and a member of UNICEF's global Digital Youth Mental Health Expert Network.

We'd never met, and she had no idea about the book I was writing. But when she spoke, I knew instantly she belonged in it. Thankfully, she agreed to be interviewed.

When I asked what she wanted to change in the mental health system, she told me,

> *I think part of our problem in mental health and traditional health services is that we have always done what we've always done. We know it doesn't work, but we're too afraid to go off script. So we rely on the individual to go off script at their own risk, which I think is inherently riskier than guiding people to the myriad of other evidence-based or evidence-informed things that they could test and try.*

We're trying to play it safe, but it's actually quite risky.

Taimi works in the field she's in because of her own mental health challenges in her teens and 20s. Her situation became dire, and by the time she was 30, she realised she needed to do something. The traditional system had become a crutch, helping her to survive (just), but certainly not to thrive. The message she'd been given was that treatments could help her stay 'okay', but that she was always going to struggle. What a thing to tell someone so early in their adult life.

Taimi decided she wanted to climb out, and to do that she needed to try things that weren't in the standard playbook—the playbook she'd been operating from unsuccessfully for over a decade. So she started experimenting. She tested everything from heavily researched interventions to alternative practices.

Some things worked. Some didn't. Meditation? Not for her. Talking therapy? Helpful, but limited. Indigenous healing that connected body, spirit and trauma release? Transformational.

Over time, Taimi built a personal 'toolbox' of what worked, always reminding others that her results were her results. It was an N-of-1 experiment, and others needed to run their own. She shared what she knew about the evidence (or lack of it), and encouraged people to explore and observe for themselves.

Rather than getting frustrated that prescribed treatments weren't working for her, or beating herself up because she wasn't doing it right, she tested things and gathered data. Now, in her role as Mental Health Commissioner for South Australia, she's encouraging others to do the same thing.

None of this is about throwing out evidence-based treatment or ignoring professional advice. It's about working with clinicians to personalise your approach, not going DIY on things that carry serious risk.

If ever there was a space where people are reluctant to experiment and take risks, it's the realm of mental health. The cost of failure can literally be life and death. This is why I chose to interview Taimi for this chapter. If we want change, but also want certainty, we need to create the right conditions to experiment, while maintaining a strong enough sense of safety to act. For practitioners and mental health professionals, like for the rest of us, it's tempting to stay within the bounds of what's common, even if it's not working. It feels risky to test something new.

The irony is that avoiding risk doesn't make you safer. It makes you stuck.

Familiar isn't always safe

Doubling-down on what you know, doing what you've always done, often feels safer because it's familiar and it's defensible. This need for safety is visible in individuals and plays out in workplaces. It's rife in politics and it's limiting our healthcare systems.

I've witnessed it firsthand through my dad's struggles with mental illness and addiction. He has seen the same psychiatrist for more than a decade, repeating a cycle of the same interventions, moving in and out of the same treatment facility, only to come out and fall back into the same pattern over and over again. And, still, they double-down.

I used to feel hope when he went in for treatment. Now, instead of it feeling like a place of potential recovery, it feels like respite. It offers a pause from the chaos of not knowing whether he's safe. It's not progress, just a break.

You've likely heard the saying that insanity is doing the same thing over and over and expecting a different result. But in mental health, that story isn't rare. It feels safer to prescribe what we know than to try something new.

But just because it's familiar, doesn't make it safe.

Guardrails for growth

Unfortunately, you can't eliminate uncertainty before you move. But you can create conditions that ease it, and do some due diligence to minimise the risk. When I asked Taimi how she defines safe experimentation, she told me, 'It's about giving people the tools and support to do it well'.

This became the organising idea for this chapter. Safe experimentation is structured curiosity. It's learning with boundaries. These boundaries aren't barriers but guardrails, and they're what make learning sustainable.

You can put in place the following three guardrails to mitigate risk and allow you to move in the face of uncertainty:

1. the right supporters
2. the right inputs
3. the Outcome Map.

The right supporters

Who the right people are to surround yourself in your experimental life depends on what you're experimenting with. In the case of your physical or mental health, you're going to want to experiment with the support of an open-minded, qualified and skilled practitioner. Taimi has some tips here.

> ### Encouraging safe experimentation: Notes from a Mental Health Commissioner
>
> If Taimi were coaching practitioners, this is what she'd tell them:
>
> - Build a broad toolkit of evidence-informed options.
> - Let clients choose where to start, and normalise that not everything works for everyone.

♦ Track results together.

♦ Use AI or reliable databases to explore new therapies safely.

People will experiment anyway; the question is whether they're supported to do it safely.

If you're reading this as a patient, nodding along to the experience of being frustrated with the prescription of a cycle of repeated treatments that just aren't working, you can encourage your practitioner toward an experimental approach.

Go into your appointments well researched and with as much data as you can. Taimi takes an Excel spreadsheet with her to see her GP. On it, she's tracked data relating to her symptoms, interventions and outcomes. They look at it together and design the next safe test. Her GP jokes that she does his job for him.

Clearly Taimi is an A-grade student, and not all of us are going to do this. But we can take away these tips: do your research, use reputable resources, track your data and don't be afraid to ask.

Most of us don't experiment well in isolation. Whether through a clinician, a peer, a colleague, a friend or a mentor, it's beneficial to have others to help you reflect, challenge your assumptions and steady you when you wobble.

Remember—you're looking for supports and guardrails here. Make sure you're not outsourcing your decisions, but staying connected enough that you don't disappear into your own echo chamber.

The right inputs

World-leading performance coach Alistair Horscroft has shared that 'the fastest way to fail is to take well-intentioned action on bad data'. I'm not encouraging anyone to take massive action based on nutrition advice from their favourite podcaster (you can learn that lesson from me), but you can see how easily it can happen.

We have unprecedented access to information and advice. Podcasts, TikToks, influencers and pseudo-experts are in our faces daily telling us what we should and shouldn't do. What's 'safe' and based on rigorous evidence can seem harder and harder to distinguish.

Even studies published in high-profile journals can sometimes have questionable backing, making trust feel tricky. This is one of the most compelling reasons that experimentation is necessary, but also something that makes change or progress on good information feel hard. You don't need certainty, but you do need discernment to determine the right inputs.

Before you act, ask, 'Where does this information come from?' If you're learning from social media, check the credentials of your source. Are they adequately qualified? Have they actually achieved what you're setting out to achieve? What sources are they citing? If you're doing your own research online, consider the evidence hierarchy.

The evidence hierarchy

Not all evidence is created equal. The evidence hierarchy is a widely used ranking of medical studies to determine the strength of the research. Knowing where information sits on this hierarchy helps you decide how confidently to act on it.

Here's a run-down of the evidence hierarchy, from strongest to weakest:

1. *Systematic reviews and meta-analyses:* These sit at the top of the hierarchy, combining multiple high-quality studies to show what consistently holds true across populations.

2. *Randomised controlled trials (RCTs):* These are the strongest individual studies. Participants are randomly assigned to groups, allowing researchers to identify cause and effect while minimising bias.
3. *Cohort and longitudinal studies:* These track groups over time to reveal long-term patterns and relationships. They're valuable, but can't prove causation as clearly as RCTs.
4. *Case studies and expert opinion:* These are useful for insight, but limited in scope. They show what's possible for some people, not what's probable for most.
5. *Anecdotes and personal experience:* These stories do matter and they capture what's humanly true. However, this might not necessarily be what's scientifically true.

The most powerful evidence arising from personal experience? Your own.

When trying to decide whether to give something a go, you don't need to be a scientist, but it is helpful to know where on the hierarchy your evidence sits. In a case where you want to try something emerging, new or poorly researched, ask yourself, 'Do I have enough reason and safety to test it myself?'

The next question to ask is, 'Is this compatible with my context and values?' Research tells you what's statistically effective. Context and values tell you what's personally sustainable. The most reliable experiment is one that works in the confines of your reality right now—within your resources, health, ethics and lifestyle.

Taimi told me a story about running a series of workshops in a men's shelter. In one of the workshops, they were talking about nutrition and how selenium can help with mental wellbeing. They wanted to run an experiment with it, but they couldn't afford pricey supplements. Taimi did some research and discovered that you could get your daily recommended amount of selenium by having just three brazil nuts per day. This they could afford, so they did. They ran the experiment and a month later the men reported noticing a difference. This is what it means to consider context.

To ensure you stay safely in the bounds of your own context and values when testing something new, ask:

- 'Does this make sense for my life right now?'
- 'Can I do it safely and sustainably?'
- 'Does it align with what matters to me?'

That's how you bridge evidence with experience.

The Outcome Map

Popular advice is to stay positive and visualise what's possible when trying to achieve your goals, diverting your gaze from what might happen if things don't work out. No-one wants to be labelled a pessimist. But, counterintuitively, it can be just as helpful to stare in the face of what would happen if things don't work out, as well as if they do.

I find myself asking this question of my coaching clients often when they're weighing up a big decision: 'What's the absolute worst thing that could happen?' It's incredible how often the answer is, 'I'd end up exactly back where I am now'. But in the case that's not the answer, sometimes articulating the worst-case scenario takes the sting out of it.

Stoic philosopher Seneca famously said: 'We suffer more often in imagination than in reality.' Ancient Stoics like Seneca practised *premeditatio malorum*, or 'premeditation of evils', which involved contemplating potential hardships to become mentally prepared for them. The Outcome Map is the version of this I use with clients. It's a simple, neuroscience-informed way to bring structure to uncertainty without getting stuck in catastrophising.

The Outcome Map has three parts that work together to help you evaluate uncertainty with clarity, momentum and agency:

1. *Downside definition:* Clarifying realistic risks.
2. *Upside projection:* Naming plausible benefits.
3. *Inaction analysis:* Mapping the cost of staying stuck.

The following figure illustrates the three-part structure of the Outcome Map, aligning the brain's threat, reward and agency systems to provide a stable foundation for safely navigating uncertainty with clarity, agency and momentum. This map is one of the core tools inside the Experiment Mindset method, because when you understand your fears, your possibilities and your agency, experimentation becomes safe enough to attempt.

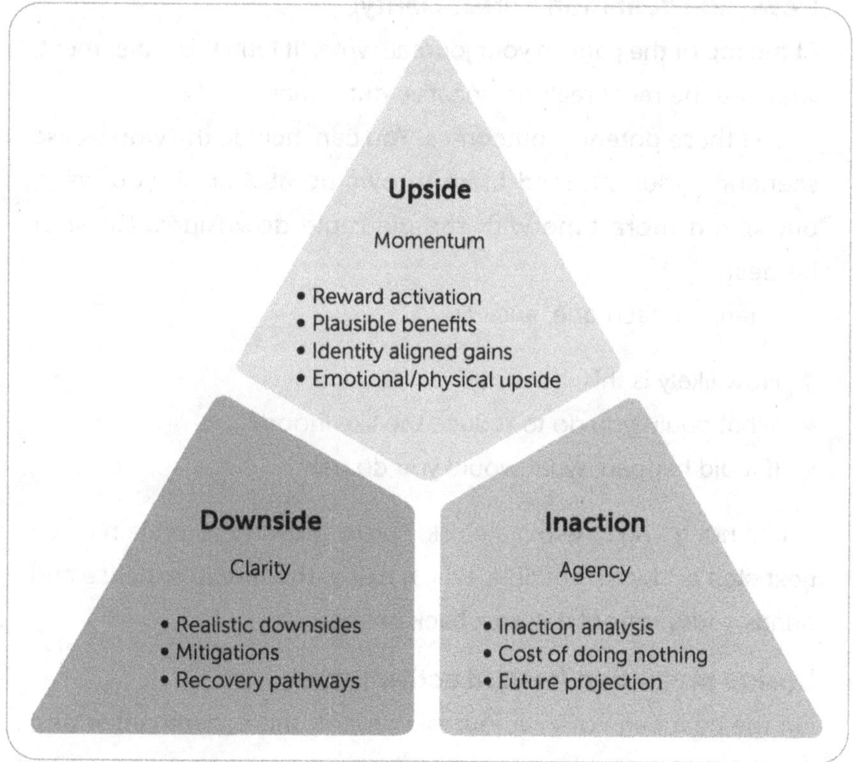

The Outcome Map

Most people never move because the risk feels undefined. The Outcome Map makes risk visible, which makes action possible.

Run through the following activity in your journal to apply the Outcome Map to an experiment you're considering. Take your time with it.

Using the Outcome Map to support safe experimentation

The Outcome Map helps you turn fear into data, and data into direction.

Downside definition (threat clarity)

At the top of the page in your journal, write, 'If I run this experiment, what are the most realistic negative outcomes?'

List these potential outcomes. You can include the worst-case scenarios your stressed brain throws up at 3 am if you want, but spend more time with the plausible downsides. Go your hardest.

Then, for each one, answer:

◆ How likely is this, honestly?

◆ What could you do to reduce the likelihood?

◆ If it did happen, what would you do next?

You're not trying to eliminate risk. You're showing your brain that a next step is always possible, which calms the threat response and brings your prefrontal cortex back online.

Upside projection (reward activation)

On the next page of your journal, write, 'If this experiment works, even partially, what becomes possible?'

List the emotional, practical, relational, financial and health benefits. Think in terms of:

◆ How might your day-to-day life improve?

◆ What might this open up in the long term?

◆ Who else could benefit if this works, even a little?

By also looking at the upside, you're giving your brain something to move towards, not just something to move away from.

Inaction analysis (agency amplifier)

On the next page, write: 'If I do nothing, what is the cost over time?'

Consider the impact emotionally, physically, financially and relationally if nothing changes. Then project these impacts out to:

◆ six months

◆ one year

◆ three years.

Ask yourself:

◆ How might you feel about yourself if nothing changes?

◆ What might this cost your health, relationships, or work?

◆ What will you wish you'd done differently, looking back?

Often, this is the page that creates the biggest aha moment. The 'risk' of trying suddenly looks smaller than the cost of staying exactly where you are.

I ran a version of this exercise using the Outcome Map with my client, Anthony.

After a successful 20-year career in healthcare management, he was ready for a change. Sick of the long hours, weekend work and grind to make money for one of Australia's corporate healthcare giants, he was considering starting his own consultancy and becoming self-employed. On the surface, this felt very risky to him. Blowing up his career and risking his high six-figure income, when he had a mortgage and two kids in private school, felt self-indulgent and dangerous.

So, running through the Outcome Map, he first wrote down his fears. These included not getting clients, burning through savings, embarrassing himself and not being able to replace his income quickly.

Then he added mitigations and recovery plans to these risks: saving three months of income before resigning, starting to consult on the side while still employed, partnering with a contact who already had a consultancy, and reminding himself that, if it all fell over, he was highly employable and could return to healthcare.

With those written down, the 'unknown' now had edges.

On the next page of his journal, he mapped the upside. This included replacing his income doing work he actually cared about, choosing who he worked with, being home in the evenings and on weekends, having the energy to look after his health, and feeling like he was building something for himself rather than just making money for other people.

And on the next page, he faced the cost of inaction. He wrote about drinking more to de-stress, barely seeing his kids, gaining weight, and feeling increasingly flat and resentful. When he projected that forward three years and imagined still being in the same role, his words were blunt: 'If I'm still doing what I'm doing, I'm going to be very annoyed with myself for wasting that time'.

He didn't suddenly feel fearless, but he did feel clearer. The risk of experimenting was no longer the biggest risk in the room.

Needless to say, Anthony ran the experiment. He started by bridging into consulting alongside his career, and he was out entirely within ten months. He never looked back.

The Outcome Map can lead to one of three things:

1. You work out the reward isn't worth the risk, and you don't run the experiment.
2. You realise the cost of inaction isn't worth the risk, and you run the experiment.
3. You realise the worst-case scenario isn't as bad as you were catastrophising in your mind, and you run the experiment.

Fear ≠ being unsafe

Experimenting safely isn't about being fearless. Throughout this book, I've emphasised that our brains aren't geared toward embracing uncertainty, so we gravitate to the known, even if it's not working for us. The process of experimentation itself helps to move in the face of fear, through the following:

- It engages the rational, thinking part of your brain, the prefrontal cortex, for curious exploration rather than obsessive overthinking.
- It reduces activation of the physiological stress response, because you know that experiments can never fail. They're simply a data-gathering exercise.
- It carves neural pathways that make it easier to confront uncertainty in the future.

The three guardrails for growth — the right supporters, the right inputs and the Outcome Map — act as a safety net for smart and sustainable experimentation.

Choice = agency = safety

When I asked Taimi what had been her biggest turning point in her own mental health, she paused and then said with conviction, 'Choice'. She went on to explain, 'For years, I thought other people had to make choices for me. Doctors, services, systems. When I realised I had a choice, that I could decide what to try and how to respond, everything shifted'.

Choice creates agency. And agency, in turn, creates safety. When people feel trapped, they freeze. When they feel trusted, they experiment. And when they experiment safely—through being supported, informed and guided—they grow.

Taimi pivoted from being treated like a victim to owning her role as curious scientist.

In the next chapter, we'll explore how you can take the Experiment Mindset into leadership, and to activate the science of personal growth at work, in your family or your community.

Reflection prompts

◆ Where in your life or work are you repeating what doesn't work because it feels safer than experimenting with something new?

◆ What's one low-risk experiment you could try instead?

11

The Experiment Mindset at work

Imagine a workplace culture where people come across a challenge and, instead of reacting with resistance or fear, they lean in with curiosity and ask, 'That's interesting. What can we learn from this?'

Previous chapters have focused on how the Experiment Mindset transforms individuals. I've outlined how you can rewire your brain, shape your environment and grow through change. But what happens when that same mindset becomes part of how teams and businesses operate? When growth stops being personal and becomes cultural?

That idea forms the basis of the most popular workshop I run in the business world at the time of writing. It's called 'How to build a high personal growth culture', and focuses on building a culture where the human, the organisation, the income and the impact can all grow together. Practically, this means creating workplaces where people feel safe enough to experiment, supported enough to grow and energised enough to perform. It's how the Experiment Mindset scales to teams and organisations, and how this language of structured curiosity becomes a refreshing new normal.

Every workshop, I ask people to think of a time when they worked with a leader, or in a team, where they came out of the experience better than they went in; a time when they genuinely grew because of the environment they were in. When I ask this, the energy in the room shifts, because this is the kind of experience that stays with you. You might like to reflect on that yourself.

When I then ask what made that experience so positive, the stories differ but the themes are always the same:

- The bar was set high.
- Someone believed in them.
- They were clear on their role and what success looked like.
- They knew what they were working toward.
- They felt like they belonged.
- The work meant something.
- They were safe to make mistakes.

These themes show up everywhere, regardless of industry, level of leadership or location. They're the conditions that allow people to grow, and the same conditions that allow the Experiment Mindset to thrive.

Then I ask a follow-up question: 'When you were part of that kind of culture, the one that helped you grow, were you lazy?'

People laugh. Across hundreds of groups, from executive teams to emerging leaders, the answer is unanimous: absolutely not. People tell me they worked hard, cared deeply and did some of their best work.

That moment changes the temperature in the room, because it reveals that when people grow, they perform. When they're trusted and stretched, when they feel seen and safe, they don't withdraw; they expand. You don't have to choose between performance and growth. You just need to understand that the conditions for growth come first — not the other way around.

Moving from high performance to high personal growth

The language of curiosity and experimentation is rare in workplaces for a reason. The traditional high-performance model, the one most organisations still default to, is built on linear growth and control. Push harder, set stricter targets, monitor output, leave no room for error and reward results. If someone knows how they achieved their targets last year, why would they test something new? If a failed project leads to punishment, why would someone risk experimentation?

For a while, the high-performance model can work. People hit their targets, the metrics look good and everyone congratulates themselves for running a tight ship. But this doesn't last. Over time, those same systems start to erode the very performance they were designed to create. People get tired, pressure turns into tension, curiosity shrinks and creativity diminishes. Eventually, you're left with burnout, low trust and disengagement. People still show up, but with less of themselves to give.

We're seeing this in the workplace data globally. According to Gallup's *State of the Global Workplace 2025* report, stress is increasing, thriving is declining and workplace engagement has begun to fall. Some companies tolerate that trade-off in the name of productivity, but even that logic doesn't hold up anymore. In Australia, productivity is declining too—and is at a 60-year low, according to the Committee for Economic Development of Australia.

At work, we borrowed the high-performance model from sport, and sport has already started to move on. Studies in sports psychology show that performance-centred coaching focused on results and comparison is linked to higher burnout, poorer mental health and lower performance. (See, for example, 'The mental health crisis in sports: The perfect storm of contemporary factors', by Claudia Reardon.) Athletes encouraged to focus on personal growth and individual skill building, and who are allowed to make mistakes? They perform better, stay healthier and sustain their performance longer. The same pattern shows up in business.

The high-performance leadership model is built on the belief that people need to be driven. My high personal growth model starts with the belief that people already are. They need the right environment to bring that drive to life. When those conditions are in place, people push themselves—not because they're scared to fail, but because they're excited about what they're working toward, they care about what they're creating and they like who they're becoming through it.

The following table outlines further differences between high-performance culture and high personal growth culture.

High-performance culture versus high personal growth culture

High-performance culture	High personal growth culture
Optimises for outcomes, targets and optics	Optimises for learning, capability and wellbeing—the conditions that produce outcomes
Relies on expertise, certainty and staying within known competencies	Normalises vulnerability, skill gaps and the reality that everyone is a work-in-progress
Creates a binary frame: succeed or fail	Creates a learning frame: test, reflect, adapt
Produces short-term spikes in performance	Produces sustained, compounding performance through continuous growth
Heightens defensiveness, impression-management and risk-avoidance	Reduces self-protection so more energy is available for creativity, experimentation and contribution
Encourages people to perform for those above them	Encourages people to contribute to something bigger than themselves
Performance pressure narrows focus and shrinks curiosity	Psychological safety expands curiosity, engagement and intrinsic motivation
Emphasises, 'Do this or we lose.'	Encourages, 'Let's learn our way to better.'
Performance is the primary goal	**Performance is the predictable by-product**

When leaders create conditions that value experimentation over perfection and growth over compliance, performance follows. People don't need to be pushed; they're pulled forward by purpose, meaning, progress and curiosity.

We need that now more than ever. The rate of technological, economic and social change means that the workforce of the future needs to be a flexible one. The old playbooks are expiring faster than we can replace them. What differentiates the organisations that thrive isn't their strategy anymore but their capacity to learn as fast as the world changes.

According to the World Economic Forum's *The Future of Jobs Report 2025*, the core skills required in the current work environment are:

- analytical thinking
- resilience, flexibility and agility
- leadership and social influence
- creative thinking
- motivation and self-awareness.

A high personal growth culture breeds these skills. It creates an environment where learning is continuous, experimentation is normal, critical thinking is celebrated and growth is shared. It's not just a nicer way to work; it's the only way to stay relevant—because when people grow, the organisation grows with them.

The Experiment Mindset has become a career superpower.

An experimental culture in action

I introduced long-term client and technology engineer James Galdes in chapter 9. As an expert in tech strategy and architecture, James led South Australia's COVID-19 response from the front line. When the pandemic hit, his team was tasked with something that, under normal government conditions, would have taken years: a functioning digital system to support the state's public health effort, tracking people's movements and identifying exposure chains.

They faced several challenges, including ensuring people complied, designing for accessibility, handling privacy concerns and processing huge volumes of data, all while coordinating between at least three government agencies that 'don't typically work that well together'. The team's target was to deliver a working system inside three weeks, an almost unthinkable time frame in government.

They didn't have time for long change programs or layers of sign-off. The usual machinery of government, the committees, the policies and the documentation, had to move aside for something more direct. 'We didn't have time to get it perfect', James told me. 'We just had to get it working, and then make it better every day.'

Once live, the system worked. They quickly iterated, adding test bookings, integrating with pathology reports, and later building a home-quarantine app that used geolocation and face verification to check compliance and free up police resources. The app evolved from a compliance tool into a platform that also supported people's mental health and symptom monitoring. 'We shipped different versions of the app as we trialled concepts', James said. 'It evolved a lot as we learned in real time.'

In total, the entire COVID-19 tech response took around three months, and South Australia's innovation was later adopted nationally.

James reflected that none of this would have been possible under normal conditions:

> *If we tried to build that now, it would take two years. But during COVID-19, our risk tolerance increased massively. We built things in a way that, if we made a mistake, we could fix it fast. We stopped over-engineering. Overthinking had diminishing returns. The best way to learn was to release, observe and adapt.*

The conditions were extreme, but in many ways they were ideal for the Experiment Mindset to thrive. The team worked cross-functionally and in real time. They built, tested, learned and improved based on live feedback. Risk tolerance expanded overnight, not because risk disappeared, but because the cost of waiting was higher than the cost of trying.

Tech engineers have a slight advantage when it comes to experimentation. They already work in cycles of testing, iteration and continuous improvement. But this was different. This wasn't just technical agility; it was cultural. The pressure stripped everything back to its essentials: clarity of purpose, autonomy to act and a shared commitment to learn fast.

Once the immediate crisis passed, however, James noticed how quickly organisations returned to the illusion of safety. They went back to plans, hierarchies and fixed processes. When he moved on to leading his next team, he made a deliberate choice not to lose what that period had taught him. That's when James and I started working together to strengthen his leadership, and establish a team culture with an embedded Experiment Mindset.

It wasn't easy. Although James came to me wanting to emulate the 'day one' startup mentality of flexible giants such as Amazon, the organisation he landed at next had a strong 100-year history of a very conservative approach to management. Helping James to establish a high personal growth culture within his pocket of the organisation took using the very mindset we wanted to encourage in his team. In other words, James needed an Experiment Mindset, where he could test his leadership approaches, fail safely, reflect through our coaching on his learnings and then adapt accordingly.

The process of building and leading a high personal growth culture uses the same three levers used in creating the conditions for your own growth: environment, psychology and physiology. You just pull them in a particular way.

In the next section, we'll explore exactly how to pull those levers, and in doing so design environments, shape mindsets and harness energy so growth becomes a cultural norm.

Creating a high personal growth culture

Every culture, whether it's a business, a family or a friendship group, grows through a mix of three forces:

1. how safe people feel (physiology)
2. how they think (psychology)
3. the context they're in (environment).

Together, these forces form the three levers for growth, building a practical structure for creating workplaces where experimentation feels safe, learning feels natural and performance becomes a side effect. Each lever unlocks a different dimension of growth, but it's the interplay between them that creates a culture where the Experiment Mindset can truly take root and thrive.

When leaders know how to work with these levers intentionally, they can build cultures that don't just survive change but also evolve through it. These same levers exist in every relationship you're part of. You don't need to run a team to use them. You're already shaping culture every time you give feedback, ask a question or choose how to respond under pressure.

If you are a part of a team, have a look at the three levers for growth, and the conditions required in each, as outlined in the following figure, and work out which one needs the most work for the Experiment Mindset to thrive in your culture.

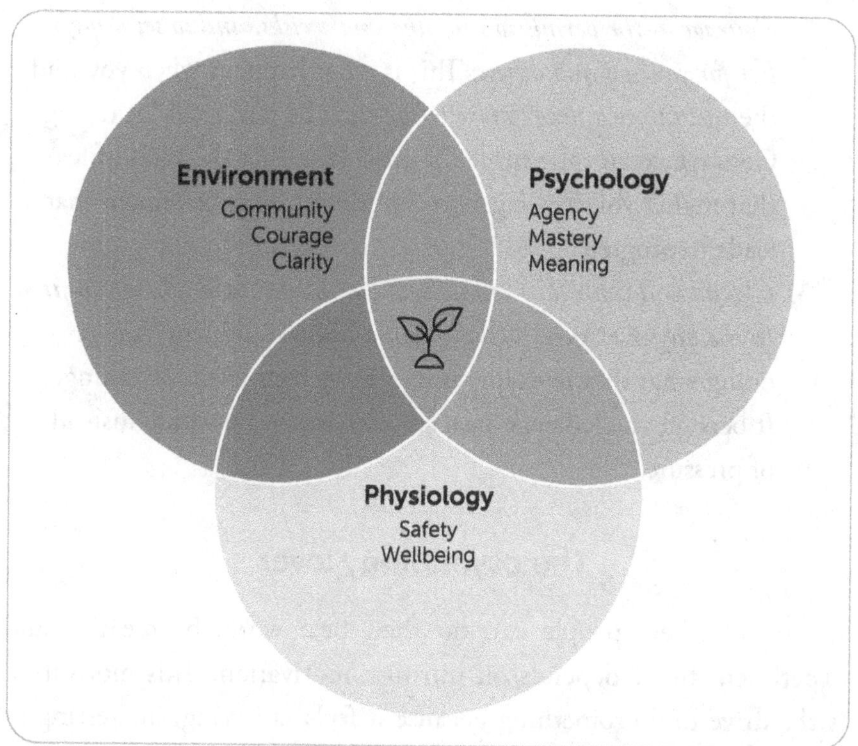

The three levers for a high personal growth culture

The environment lever

The environment we work in shapes how we show up, influencing our creativity, courage and ability to experiment. When people feel part of something, when they understand where they fit and why it matters, they grow faster and perform better.

Three environmental forces make that possible:

1. *Community—the sense of belonging and shared purpose:* This is that feeling you get when you're part of something bigger than you and you know the people around you have your back. You know you can bring ideas, doubts or failures to the table and still feel seen and accepted.

2. *Courage—the permission to take smart risks, and to set a high
   bar for yourself and others:* This is what happens when you and
   the rest of your team know you won't be punished for trying.
   Courage creates the space for growth so that the kind of fear
   that makes you freeze gets replaced with nerve-citement that
   leads to progress.
3. *Clarity and context—knowing what matters and where you fit
   in the bigger picture:* When people understand why they're
   doing what they're doing, uncertainty feels less threatening.
   It becomes a challenge instead of chaos and purpose instead
   of pressure.

The psychology lever

A culture where people can do their best work, be creative and
experiment freely depends on intrinsic motivation. This motivation
is the drive to do something because it feels satisfying, interesting or
meaningful.

The opposite is extrinsic motivation—being driven by external
rewards or fear of punishment (or the old carrot-and-stick approach).
This might be bonuses dangled in front, with consequences waiting
behind. This approach works in the short term, but it can kill curiosity,
creativity and joy over time.

Dan Pink explores this deeply in his book *Drive*, drawing on
over 40 years of research into human motivation. I've adapted
his model through my own coaching and consulting work, after
experimenting with what language and framing people connect
the most with.

I've now landed on three psychological conditions that spark and
sustain intrinsic motivation.

Agency

Agency is the sense that you have choice and influence, and that your voice and decisions matter. It's not about total freedom; it's about feeling trusted enough to do things your way.

We crave agency from the time we can talk. In my house, this shows up every night around 7 pm. If I say to my youngest son, 'Charlie, can you please go and have a shower?' he'll either ignore me or flat-out refuse. But if I ask, 'Would you like a bath or a shower tonight?' he's already running the taps.

That need for choice doesn't disappear when we grow up. We just get less aware of how much it affects our motivation.

Mastery

Mastery is the feeling that you're improving in something that matters, and that you have the space to grow and the support to get there. For people to experience mastery, they need visible room to grow. This might be a pathway that they're on or that is visible, a challenge to tackle or a mentor who believes in them. As a leader, that might mean helping someone see how their current role connects to their longer term goals, or giving them a project that stretches them just enough to learn something new.

Growth has to be personal to be powerful. You (and members of your team) are far more likely to commit to an experiment when it aligns with your own vision of who you want to become and what you care about getting better at. If someone offers me a growth opportunity in spread sheeting, for example, it's not going to motivate me. Offer me an opportunity to keynote in front of a new and bigger audience? I'm all in. It's unique and individualised. Working out where this mastery and growth could happen requires an N-of-1 approach.

Meaning

Dan Pink's work uses the word 'purpose' here. And while conceptually I agree, what I'm seeing out in the personal and professional development world is that the big push for purpose is actually making people stuck. Thinking that we all have one big purpose in life, and we all need to be in search of it, can feel overwhelming. And even if the idea of 'one big purpose' were true, not all of us are going to find our life's purpose through our work.

Meaning, on the other hand, is absolutely accessible. I was invited to work with a tech team once to help improve staff engagement, which was painfully low. When I spoke to the team, it became clear why. Their goalposts kept moving. Three times in the previous year, they'd been building products that were cut before they ever reached the user. You can see why their motivation was slipping. They'd been pouring their hearts and hours into work that never made a dent.

People don't need constant praise, or even constant success. But they do need to know that their work counts for something, and that it has weight and consequence. That's meaning.

The physiology lever

When focusing on the physiology lever in high personal growth cultures, safety and wellbeing are the important factors.

Safety

Such a thing as 'post traumatic growth' is possible. But that's really not what I want for you at work. Here, I'm talking about the kind of growth that comes from safety. It's almost impossible to experiment, create or stretch when your nervous system is in survival mode. If your body, your bank account or your workplace feel unsafe, your brain's priority shifts from learning to protecting.

In the workplace, safety comes in a few different forms:

- *Physical safety:* This is the most basic need to feel secure in your body and your environment. It's hard to focus on growth if you're chronically sleep-deprived, in pain, or constantly exposed to risk or conflict. Your physiology needs stability before it can handle stretch.
- *Financial safety:* This safety comes from knowing that your basic needs are met and that your future feels predictable enough to take risks. You can't innovate when you're one invoice away from panic. Security doesn't have to mean luxury, but it does mean not living with constant threat.
- *Psychological safety:* This form of safety has deservingly found its way up there (along with wellbeing) as the workplace culture buzzword for the last decade. Harvard professor Amy Edmondson's research across industries shows that teams with higher psychological safety may report more errors, but they also learn faster, solve problems sooner and ultimately deliver stronger results. When people feel safe to tell the truth (which is likely why they report more errors, not because they're making more) performance accelerates. This is the feeling that you can speak up, be honest, trust the people you're working with and make mistakes without fear of humiliation or punishment. It's the kind of safety that lets people tell the truth, ask for help and take creative risks.

Psychological safety can be built via the environmental and psychological conditions for growth—that is, community, courage, clarity, agency, mastery and meaning. The levers work together. You can't demand courage if someone feels unsafe; instead, you create courage through safety.

I coached a CEO once who was frustrated that her team came to her with every single problem, and that they weren't taking agency and being creative. She thought they were lacking 'get up and go'. What I discovered was that she needed development in her self-regulation. She would fly off the handle when she was stressed, and her team just didn't know what they were going to get when they walked in the room on any given day. They weren't operating with courage, because they didn't feel safe.

If people are constantly scanning for threats, their energy goes to self-protection instead of contribution. But when safety is in place, when people feel steady, supported and trusted, they can redirect that energy into learning, experimentation and growth.

Wellbeing

Workplace wellbeing is a hot topic, with global spending on workplace wellness set to top US$94.6 billion by 2026 (according to a MarketsandMarkets report). Sadly, all that spending isn't translating into results. I have a six-year-old boy who still believes that bandaids instantly fix his scrapes; however, this trick doesn't work for us in the workplace. Bandaid solutions such as after-work yoga, mindfulness classes, apps, and 'lunch and learns' aren't going to cut it. Indeed, a study by Oxford University's William Fleming (published in *Industrial Relations Journal*) found that these kinds of initiatives have no significant impact on wellbeing or job satisfaction. In fact, sometimes they can even make things worse. The unpopular and inconvenient truth is that the most effective way to improve workplace wellbeing is by reducing stress, rather than adding ways to cope with it.

Fleming's study points out that it is possible to improve wellbeing at work by focusing on more structural aspects of work. These include improving pay and providing secure contracts (safety), offering flexibility and control over where and when people work (agency), and providing opportunities for growth (mastery). Sound familiar?

Leading a high personal growth culture

As a leader, whether of a business, a team, a family or a friendship, you have the ability to create an environment where people leave better than they came in. And if you can, you should. The three levers of environment, psychology and physiology work together to create a model that makes growth contagious. They're designed to build a culture where learning is normal and experimentation is safe, and where people feel like they're a part of something and are proud of who they're becoming through their work. That's what a high personal growth culture is. It's what the future of leadership requires, and how we'll keep evolving in a world that won't stop changing.

Don't feel like you're in a position to influence the three levers? Short of leaving this book on your bosses desk (also recommended), your strongest tool of influence is through role modelling. Share your experiments out loud. Let people know when you're failed and learned. And if someone comes to you feeling stuck, ask them how they can test and learn.

Living an experimental life will inspire you. But it will also inspire those around you. Don't keep it to yourself.

Reflection prompts

- Where can you create more agency in your own life? And if you lead others, where can you offer it?
- What's one skill you'd like to master in the next 12 months?
- Who around you could use a little more space to grow?
- Where does your work feel meaningful right now? If it doesn't, what would make it so?
- If you're a leader, how can you highlight the impact of your team's work?
- What kind of safety do you still need to build—physical, financial or psychological—to grow into what comes next?

12

Living experimentally

I'm writing this book and launching an absorbent activewear startup—JumpProof—at the same time. I have absolutely no idea whether either of these experiments is going to work out. I've invested months of my time in writing this book, and I don't even know if anyone is going to get far enough along to read these words. I've invested tens of thousands of dollars in JumpProof, and I have no idea if anyone will buy a single pair.

When you live an experimental life, there is no certainty. If the outcome is certain, it's not an experiment. All you can do is choose to run experiments where the learnings you'll gain, even if the experiment doesn't go to plan, are worth the risk.

If no-one but my own mum reads this book, I've learned enough from writing it about myself and my work that the pay-off is worth the cost. The clarity I've gained about my methodology, the conversations it's sparked and the way it's forced me to articulate what I've been doing instinctively for years all make the process worth it.

The process of bringing JumpProof to life—building a product that is genuinely helpful to millions of women, and seeing the people I've engaged to work on the project falling in love with the vision like I have—is also worth it.

If you're reading this in five years, you'll know what happened next. That's kind of beautiful.

I'm not the same person I was when I started either of these experiments. Whether they 'succeed' or not, I've already grown, and that's what living experimentally does. *It changes you through the doing, not through the outcome.*

What living experimentally actually looks like

Not all experiments are going to be mammoth ones like mine. In fact, they're usually not. Living experimentally isn't something you do occasionally when you're stuck or when it's time to take a leap. The mindset becomes your default operating system, and the way you move through the world day to day.

This approach is not about being reckless or chaotic; it's about being intentional with your uncertainty, choosing to test rather than overthink and to learn rather than to know.

When you're living an experimental life, you'll notice some clues. In decision making, you'll notice that instead of agonising over whether something is the 'right' choice, you frame it as a test. 'I'm going to try this for three months and see what I learn.' The pressure comes off immediately because you're not committing forever; you're just gathering data and deciding what to do next.

This can work for decisions that feel bigger and scarier too. If I've got a client making a big career decision, and feeling nervous but also excited about making the shift, I always ask the same question: 'If you make this move and in 12 months you know it wasn't the right one, what's the worst that could happen?' Usually, the answer is that they'll end up right back where they are now, looking for their next career move but with a little more experience under their belt.

Treat the shift like a test, rather than a complete life overhaul.

When you come up against a failure, which you inevitably will if you're stretching enough, you'll notice a change too. An experiment not working out stops being a signal that you're not good enough, and starts being helpful new information. Your language shifts from 'I failed' to 'I learned'—even if it still stings for a while.

One of my coaching clients, Sarah, had been stuck in analysis paralysis about whether to leave her corporate marketing role and go out on her own. We designed an experiment that allowed her to take on a couple of projects for businesses she knew well while she was still employed (with her employer's blessing) to test whether she actually enjoyed the work. One project went great and the other one was a disaster. The client was all over the place, the scope kept expanding and she ended up working crazy hours for barely any money to get the job done.

Once, this 'disaster' might have sent her spiralling. She would have taken it as proof she wasn't cut out for working for herself and retreated back to safety. She didn't, however, because we'd framed it as an experiment, with the learning being the point. Sarah learned that she needed to be more careful about setting scope and making the boundaries clear right from the get-go. She also learned that she absolutely loved the work when it was with the right client. She didn't leave her job until two years later, working for herself on the side until then. By the time she took the leap, she knew she could do it, because she'd done it.

I notice this kind of response in my own life a lot. I'm part-owner in a family business, and I'm known as the level-headed one. I know that this is because when we come up against challenges or failures, my business partners are only looking at the failure and I'm looking beyond it. I'm thinking about how we use the learning to evolve and move forward, and it steadies the whole ship.

When an opportunity lands in front of you, with an Experiment Mindset you'll notice that instead of needing to feel certain before you say yes, you get curious. You start asking better questions—not 'Will this work?' or 'Can I do this?' but 'What could I learn from this?'

A few years ago, my friend Amy Springhall and I were invited to MC Adelaide's Mother's Day Classic. This event is held every year in the Adelaide parklands, with thousands of participants dressed up in pink coming together to start their Mother's Day running and walking along the River Torrens and raising money for breast cancer research. I'd run in this event before, and I knew that they usually had local celebrities and seasoned MCs on the mics so it felt like a huge stretch, but Amy and I were ecstatic to be invited and knew it was worth a try. We've just been invited back for our fourth year in a row and it's one of our favourite days on the calendar. We didn't know we could do it until we did it, and it turns out we're great at it and we love it.

You'll also notice the Experiment Mindset in how you talk about your life. You stop using definitive statements like, 'This is just who I am' and start using the language of evolution about who you're becoming. You'll know your identity isn't set in the past; it's calibrated to your horizon. You'll talk about where you're heading, not where you've been.

The big shift that you'll notice is that instead of needing to know before you move, you'll want to find out as you go. Your lived experience will become more valuable to you than someone else's opinion. You'll gain a sense of agency and momentum because you won't need to wait to be told, read the right book or do the right course. You'll trust yourself.

Incredible freedom comes with this, because most people are stuck trying to know before they move and it stunts their growth. They want certainty before they take the first step, and they want to see the whole staircase before they climb. Without this, they hesitate or stay put.

Living experimentally means you're comfortable moving without knowing, and you trust that clarity will emerge through acting, not before it. You trust that you'll figure it out along the way, and the more you do it the more that trust will grow.

Filtering the experiments you choose

Now, an Experiment Mindset doesn't mean being reckless. I hope you've learned that by now because you know how to be intentional about which experiments you run and how you set them up. At the same time, though, you're not waiting for perfect information or guaranteed outcomes.

One potential trap you might find yourself in (I know I do sometimes) is that once you adopt this mindset, suddenly everything becomes a possible experiment. You could experiment with your career, your relationships, your morning routine, your communication style, where you live, how you exercise, what you eat and how you structure your week. The possibilities are endless.

I gave you some frameworks in the chapters in part III, when we were looking at how to design your experiments. As you move on to make experimentation a way of life, these frameworks begin to fall in to the background as just the way you think and operate. That's what a mindset is.

The way to know what to experiment with in a way that feels more like instinct and less like work is to use filters—and I suggest three.

Horizon alignment

Remember the Horizon Builder from chapter 3? Every experiment should be pointing you in the direction of the person you're becoming and the life you want to build. It should be moving you towards your horizon.

If your horizon includes, 'I want to be surrounded by energising and engaging people who are building things', for example, and you're considering an experiment that involves working from home more, ask yourself whether this is likely to move you toward or away from that experience.

If your horizon includes, 'I want to be around people who challenge me to grow' and you're considering joining a new community, ask whether this group of people matches that vision.

Your horizon acts like a compass. It doesn't tell you exactly where to step, but it tells you which direction to face.

Risk to learning ratio

Don't ask, 'Will this succeed?' Ask, 'What will I learn, and is that learning worth what I'm risking?' In other words, are the lessons worth the cost, even if the experiment fails?

When I decided to pursue JumpProof, I knew there was a real chance it wouldn't work. The activewear market is saturated, I had no experience in product development or e-commerce, and I was stepping into a completely new domain. But I also knew that even if it failed, I'd learn:

- how to build a product from concept to launch
- how to work with manufacturers and suppliers
- how to test a market and validate an idea
- how to lead a creative project outside my usual field of expertise
- whether I enjoyed entrepreneurship in a product-based business.

The experiment also fulfilled this niggling sense I've always had that I wanted to build a brand, and provided me with purpose because I was helping to solve the problem of bladder leakage during exercise that one in three women have and never talk about. Essentially, I just couldn't stand not finding out what might happen.

Those lessons alone were worth the risk. Even if no-one buys a single pair of leggings or undies, I won't look back and think, *That was a waste*. I'll look back and see growth. I already can.

Compare that to an experiment with a high cost but minimal learning. If I invested the same amount of money in trying to replicate someone else's business model in a domain I wasn't curious about or didn't care about, just because it seemed profitable, that wouldn't pass the risk-to-learning filter. Even if it succeeded, I wouldn't have learned anything that mattered to me.

How does it feel?

The best experiments live in that sweet spot where you're equal parts excited and terrified. If you're just excited, the experiment might not stretch you enough and if you're just afraid, you might be forcing yourself down a path that isn't right for you. The experiments that change you are the ones where you think, *I have no idea if I can do this, but I really want to find out.*

That balance of feeling excited and afraid is your signal to pay attention to the experiment, even if it's faint.

When I signed the contract with Wiley to write this book, I felt both. I was excited because I'd wanted to write a book for years, I wanted to see if I could do it and I had something important to share. But I was also afraid because I had no idea if I could actually do it or if anyone would read it.

That combination told me it was the right experiment to run.

Knowing when to quit and when to persist

Living experimentally doesn't mean you never question your commitment or bail at the first sign of difficulty. The growth requires the struggle, but sometimes you need to know when to call it quits.

End the experiment when:

- *You've gathered the data you needed:* Sometimes the point of an experiment is simply to answer a question. Once you have your answer, you're done. You don't need to keep going just because you started.
- *The cost is outweighing the learning:* Every experiment has a cost, including time, money, energy and opportunity cost. As long as what you're learning feels worth it, keep going. But when the scales tip, and only a very honest you will know that, and you're investing more than you're gaining, it's time to stop.
- *It's no longer aligned with your horizon:* As you grow, your horizon shifts. An experiment that made perfect sense six months ago might not fit who you're becoming now. It's not a failure; it's evolution.
- *You're not curious anymore; you're just grinding:* There's a difference between productive struggle (the kind that grows you) and pointless suffering (the kind that just depletes you). Another learning from Alistair Horscroft is that if an experiment has shifted from 'this is hard but I'm learning or heading somewhere meaningful' to 'I'm just forcing myself through this', pay attention. Curiosity is fuel. When it's gone, you're running on fumes.

Keep going when:

- *You're in the messy middle:* Every experiment has a predictable phase in which it gets hard before it gets good. You've invested enough that quitting feels wasteful, but you haven't been at it long enough to see results. This is not the time to quit. This is the time to trust the process.

- *You're learning, even if you're struggling:* If you're still gathering data, still noticing patterns and still evolving your approach, the experiment is working. Struggle doesn't mean you're failing; it means you're growing.
- *The original question hasn't been answered yet:* If you set out to test whether something works for you and you genuinely don't know yet, keep going. Give the experiment enough time to generate real data.

The key is being honest with yourself about the experiment and its benefits.

The compounding effect

When you're in the middle of an experiment, you can't predict how it will compound. Every experiment I've run has prepared me for the next one, often in ways I couldn't have predicted at the time.

When I said yes to that leader-as-coach program a decade ago, I thought I was just learning coaching skills. I had no idea it would lead me to Noosa to study, which would lead me to completely reshape my career, which would eventually lead me to here.

Each experiment builds capabilities, connections and clarity that become the foundation for what's next. Every experiment builds your momentum toward who you're becoming.

Your non-linear growth path feels random but it isn't; it's more like compound interest. Every experiment, whether it 'succeeds' or 'fails', deposits something into your account. Over time, those deposits add up in ways you can only see when you look backward.

You can't engineer this kind of compounding. You can only create the conditions for it by staying in motion, staying curious and paying attention to what emerges.

Permission to make it your own

Living experimentally looks different for everyone. For me, it looks like launching businesses and writing books and saying yes to stages I'm not sure I'm ready for. For you, it might look like micro-experiments in how you show up at work, testing a new boundary in a relationship, saying no to something you'd normally say yes to or speaking up in a meeting when you'd normally stay quiet.

The scale doesn't matter, the mindset does.

My client Brent was struggling to connect with his family when he got home from work because his mind stayed so busy. He experimented with meditating for 10 minutes per day during weekday mornings to learn if he could quiet his brain. This helped him feel calmer at work, but that feeling didn't extend to the evening. He shifted the experiment to sitting in his car doing the meditation before he drove home, and that significantly helped.

That seems pretty small, but it's changed how Brent feels about himself and his work, and it's actually helped his relationship with his wife as much as with his kids. The shift didn't come from reading a parenting book; it came from running a test.

You met another of my clients, Cara, back in chapter 1. She built a business in the care sector, only to learn that while she loved the growth phase, she didn't love the destination. Her experiments to get unstuck didn't look like mine.

She experimented with delegating certain aspects off her plate, which lightened the load but didn't light her spark. She experimented with bringing a business manager in, which changed the type of work she was doing but didn't make her feel any different at work. She experimented with taking an extended break and travelling the country in her caravan. This gave her the space she needed to really reflect. She decided to sell her business, but she made this decision with all the data she needed to know that it was the right move. Experimenting made it safer.

She didn't wait for clarity to move; instead, she moved through testing, learning and adapting, and the clarity came. That's living experimentally.

Another friend of mine, Lisa, is in her 60s. She's not changing careers or chasing some dramatic transformation, but she is experimenting. She's testing whether she enjoys volunteering (she does), whether she wants to reconnect with old friends (some yes, some no), and whether she's ready to date again after her husband passed away (still figuring that out).

Living experimentally isn't age-specific or domain-specific. It's a way of moving through life that says, 'I don't need to know. I just need to be willing to find out'. It's for anyone who isn't done growing.

You get to make this your own. So choose experiments that add value to your life just through running them. Choose the kind that make you part excited and part afraid, and the ones where the lessons are as valuable as the pay-off.

That's what living an experimental life feels like. You're not attached to the destination or the outcome because your goal is the growth. Your goal is coming out the other side wiser than you went in.

The magic is that somewhere along the way, you realise you're not the same person who started. You've become someone who knows how to grow yourself, someone who trusts yourself to figure it out, and someone who sees uncertainty as possibility instead of threat.

You've become your own best experiment.

You now have everything you need: the science that explains how growth actually works, an understanding of the levers you're working with, the method for designing and running experiments, the tools for gathering data and building wisdom, and the understanding that growth isn't about following someone else's path. It's about building your own.

What you do next is up to you.

You don't need to know how it will turn out, you don't need to feel ready and you don't need a permission slip (but consider this yours). You just need to be willing to find out.

The experiments don't stop and neither does the growth.

Close this book, open your journal, look to your horizon and design your first experiment.

Reflection prompts

- When you face a decision, do you agonise over whether it's 'right' or do you frame it as something you can test?
- What experiment are you avoiding because you're waiting to feel certain first?
- What's one thing that makes you equal parts excited and terrified? Why haven't you started yet?
- Are you in the 'messy middle' where you need to persist, or are you grinding through something you're no longer curious about?
- If you closed this book right now and designed one experiment for tomorrow, what would it be?

Conclusion

Early in this book I told you that we're drowning in insight and starving for change; that despite spending billions of dollars on personal development, we're more overwhelmed, burned out and uncertain than we've ever been. But the problem was never that we didn't know enough. It was that we've been trying to think our way into becoming someone different, when the only way to actually become someone different is to do something different and learn from what happens.

You can't think your way into confidence, you can't plan your way into courage and you can't read your way into wisdom. You have to gather the kind of experience that changes you from the inside out, and updates not just what you know but also who you are.

That's what the Experiment Mindset method has given you: a way to move before you're ready, to learn as you go and to build a life that evolves with you instead of leaving you behind. It's a way of being in the world that says uncertainty isn't something to eliminate but something to work with. Instead of not knowing being a sign you're not ready, it's a sign you're exactly where growth happens.

The fundamental growth shifts

If you've stayed with me this far, somewhere along the way you've made seven fundamental shifts in how you approach your own growth. These shifts change not only what you do but also how you see yourself and what becomes possible.

From goal setting to horizon setting

You're no longer chasing fixed outcomes that might be obsolete by the time you reach them. And nor are you building five-year plans in a world that changes every five months. You've set a direction instead of a destination, and given yourself a true north that keeps you oriented without locking you into a path that no longer fits. You know where you're heading and you're flexible about how you get there, which means you can pivot, adapt and evolve without feeling like you've failed every time the plan changes.

From fixed identity to evolving identity

You've stopped saying things like, 'This is just who I am' as if your identity was carved in stone at 25 and you're stuck with it forever. Instead, you've started asking, 'Who am I becoming?' and you understand now that your identity isn't something you discover once and defend forever. It's something you update through experience. Every experiment gives you new evidence about who you can be, and you've learned to treat your sense of self as something alive and responsive rather than rigid and immovable.

From information to wisdom

You've moved from endlessly collecting information to actually doing something with it, and you understand now that reading another book or listening to another podcast won't change you, but running an experiment and honestly reflecting on what happened will. You've stopped mistaking the consumption of insight for the cultivation of transformation, and stopped letting high-quality procrastination masquerade as progress. You know now that intelligence gathers information, but wisdom knows what to do with it.

From control to curiosity

You've stopped trying to eliminate all uncertainty before you move, and stopped waiting for the moment when you feel completely ready and the path is completely clear. You've learned to work with uncertainty instead of against it, and lean into the discomfort of not knowing rather than running from it. When something doesn't go to plan, you don't spiral into self-doubt anymore, or at least not for as long. You get curious instead. You ask what the data is telling you, what you can learn and what to test next.

From failure to data

When something doesn't work out the way you hoped, you don't spiral into shame or self-blame anymore. You gather the data, you reflect on what it's telling you, and you design your next experiment. You've learned that failure isn't final; it's feedback.

From fixing what hurts to changing what matters

You're no longer putting bandaids over symptoms or chasing the next productivity hack that promises to fix everything if you just wake up early enough or build the right morning routine. You understand the three levers of environment, physiology and psychology, and you know which one to pull when you're stuck. You're working with your whole system—with your brain and your body, your mind and your context—instead of fighting against parts of yourself while trying to force change in others.

From fear to freedom

You've learned that fear isn't a sign you shouldn't do something but, often, a sign that your identity is stretching and you're stepping into a version of yourself you haven't inhabited yet. You've stopped waiting to feel fearless and started moving anyway, because you've discovered that confidence doesn't arrive before action, like some kind of prerequisite, but comes from the lived experience of knowing you can handle what happens after. You've learned that freedom isn't the absence of fear; it's the willingness to move through it.

These fundamental shifts have created the building blocks of your Experiment Mindset.

One last thing...

I'm writing this conclusion while sitting in my office looking over our little farm, and I have absolutely no idea whether this book will do what I hope it will do. I don't know whether it will land with you the way I want it to, or whether anyone will read these words and feel something shift inside them, some small opening of possibility where before there was only uncertainty or fear or 'stuckness'.

I wrote this book anyway, because the experiment was worth running regardless of the outcome.

I learned things about myself I couldn't have learned any other way. I clarified my thinking in ways that have already changed how I work with my clients, how I show up in my own life and how I talk to my kids about trying new things. I connected with people I never would have met. I became someone who wrote a book, which is something I've always secretly wanted to do and didn't believe I could.

The outcome didn't create that growth; the process did. The process of doing, showing up even when I didn't feel ready, gathering data, reflecting, adapting, and staying with it when it felt hard and uncertain and like maybe I'd made a terrible mistake.

That's what I want for you—not some distant future where you've 'arrived' at some imagined destination and can finally relax because you've made it, but a present where you're in motion, where you're learning and you're becoming. I want you to feel like the life you're building is actually yours, not some hand-me-down version of what you thought you were supposed to want.

Throughout these pages, you've met real people living experimental lives. Emma set her eyes on her horizon, redesigned her life and found a love for her work again. Alex learned to see setbacks as information, not verdicts. Sophie tested before she built and saved years of procrastination.

They won't talk to you about experimentation (although they say my voice in their head does). None of them will tell you they became 'fearless'. But they will tell you they became free.

They'll talk about finding joy, agency, momentum and confidence. This wasn't the confidence that they're excellent at everything and will never fail, but the confidence that when they do, they'll know how to run their next test.

The same mindset that changed their lives, and mine, is now in your hands. This is where I hand you your lab coat. You've earned it. You've set your horizon. You've looked at the three levers you can pull, psychology, physiology and environment, and where you might start. You've designed your first experiment. You've learned how to track your data, respond to feedback, iterate and evolve.

You know what to do now. Rest, celebrate and then look up. Remember that growth isn't linear and failure isn't final. It's simply a data-gathering exercise.

Your next experiment is waiting.

References and further reading

Introduction

Gallup (2025), *State of the Global Workplace 2025 Report*, Gallup.
Grand View Research (2024), *Personal Development Market (2025–2030)*, Grand View Research.

Chapter 1

Arkes, HR, & Blumer, C (1985), 'The psychology of sunk cost', *Organizational Behavior and Human Decision Processes*, 35(1), 124–140.
Brickman, P, & Campbell, DT (1971), 'Hedonic relativism and planning the good society', in Appley, MH (ed.), *Adaptation-Level Theory*, Academic Press.
Dickson, JM, et al (2017), 'An integrative study of motivation and goal regulation processes in subclinical anxiety, depression and hypomania', *Psychiatry Research*, 256, 6–12.
Duckworth, A (2016), *Grit: The Power of Passion and Perseverance*, Scribner.
Fishbach, A (2022), *Get It Done: Surprising Lessons from the Science of Motivation*, Little, Brown and Company.
Grant, A (2021), *Think Again: The Power of Knowing What You Don't Know*, Viking.
Headey, B (2008), 'Life goals matter to happiness: A revision of set-point theory' *Social Indicators Research*, 86(2), 213–231.
Ibarra, H (2003), *Working Identity: Unconventional Strategies for Reinventing Your Career*, Harvard Business School Press.

Kahneman, D (2011), *Thinking, Fast and Slow*, Farrar, Straus and Giroux.

Mckendrick, J (2024), 'AI puts the squeeze on the shrinking half-life of skills', *Forbes*.

Rose, T (2016), *The End of Average: How We Succeed in a World that Values Sameness*, HarperOne.

World Economic Forum (2025), *Future of Jobs Report 2025*, World Economic Forum.

Chapter 2

Barrett, LF (2017), *How Emotions are Made: The Secret Life of the Brain*, Houghton Mifflin Harcourt.

Clark, A (2013), 'Whatever next? Predictive brains and the future of cognitive science', *Behavioral and Brain Sciences*, 36(3), 181–204.

Cleo, G (2024), *The Habit Revolution: Simple Steps to Rewire Your Brain for Powerful Habit Change*, Murdoch Books.

Doidge, N (2007), *The Brain that Changes Itself: Stories of Personal Triumph from the Frontiers of Brain Science*, Viking.

Friston, K (2010), 'The free-energy principle: A unified brain theory?', *Nature Reviews Neuroscience*, 11(2), 127–138.

Holroyd, CB, & Yeung, N (2012), 'Motivation of extended behaviours by anterior cingulate cortex', *Trends in Cognitive Sciences*, 16(2), 122–128.

May, A (2011), 'Experience-dependent structural plasticity in the adult brain', *Trends in Cognitive Sciences*, 15(10), 475–482.

Quoidbach, J, Gilbert, DT, & Wilson, TD (2013), 'The end of history illusion', *Science*, 339(6115), 96–98.

Raichle, ME, & Gusnard, DA (2002), 'Appraising the brain's energy budget', *Proceedings of the National Academy of Sciences*, 99(16), 10237–10239.

Sagi, Y, et al (2012), 'Learning in the fast lane', *Nature Neuroscience*, 15(4), 528–536.

Sapolsky, RM (2004), *Why Zebras Don't Get Ulcers* (3rd ed), Henry Holt.

Sapolsky, RM (2015), 'Stress and the brain: Individual variability and the inverted-U', *Nature Neuroscience*, 18(10), 1344–346.

Sapolsky, RM (2017), *Behave: The Biology of Humans at Our Best and Worst*, Penguin Press.

Schwartz, JM, & Begley, S (2002), *The Mind and the Brain: Neuroplasticity and the Power of Mental Force*, HarperCollins.

Shenhav, A, Botvinick, M, & Cohen, JD (2013), 'The expected value of control: An integrative theory of anterior cingulate cortex function', *Neuron*, 79(2), 217–240.

Vassena, E, Holroyd, CB & Alexander, WH (2017), 'Computational models of anterior cingulate cortex: At the crossroads between prediction and effort', *Frontiers in Neuroscience*, 11.

Zeine, F, et al (2024), 'Awareness integration theory: A Psychological and genetic path to self-directed neuroplasticity', *Health Sciences Review*, 11, 100169.

Chapter 3

Bernstein, ES, & Turban, S (2018), 'The impact of the 'open' workspace on human collaboration', *Philosophical Transactions of the Royal Society B*, 373(1753), 20170239.

Bryan, CJ, Tipton, E, & Yeager, DS (2021), 'Behavioural science is unlikely to change the world without a heterogeneity revolution', *Nature Human Behaviour*, 5(8), 980–989.

Curran, T, & Hill, AP (2019), 'Perfectionism is increasing over time: A meta-analysis', *Psychological Bulletin*, 145(4), 410–429.

Dweck, CS (2006), *Mindset: The New Psychology of Success*, Random House.

Finkel, E (2025), *Prove It: A Scientific Guide for the Post-Truth Era*, Black Inc.

Guyatt, GH, et al (1990), 'The N-of-1 randomized controlled trial: Clinical usefulness. Our three-year experience', *Annals of Internal Medicine*, 112(4), 293–299.

Kent, JA (2023), 'Perfectionism might be hurting you. Here's how to change your relationship to achievement', Harvard Summer School.

Lillie, EO, et al (2011), 'The N-of-1 clinical trial: The ultimate strategy for individualizing medicine', *Personalized Medicine*, 8(2), 161–173.

Mirza, R, Punja, S, Vohra, S & Guyatt, G (2017), 'The history and development of N-of-1 trials', *Journal of the Royal Society of Medicine*, 110(8), 330–340.

Nahum-Shani, I, et al (2018), 'Just-in-time adaptive interventions (JITAIs) in mobile health: Key components and design principles for ongoing health behavior support', *Annals of Behavioral Medicine*, 52(6), 446–462.

Noone, J, et al (2024), 'Understanding the variation in exercise responses to guide personalized physical activity prescriptions', *Cell Metabolism*, 36(4), 702–724.

Roll, R (2012), *Finding Ultra: Rejecting Middle Age, Becoming One of the World's Fittest Men, and Discovering Myself*, Crown Publishing Group.

Schwartz, JM, & Gladding, R (2011), *You Are Not Your Brain: The 4-Step Solution for Changing Bad Habits, Ending Unhealthy Thinking, and Taking Control of Your Life*, Avery.

Wolf, G, & de Groot, M (2020), 'A conceptual framework for personal science', *Frontiers in Computer Science*, 2.

Chapter 4

Christakis, NA, & Fowler, JH (2009), *Connected: The Surprising Power of Our Social Networks and How They Shape Our Lives*, Little, Brown.

Christakis, NA, & Fowler, JH (2012), 'Social contagion theory: examining dynamic social networks and human behavior', *Statistics in Medicine*, 32(4), 556–577.

Jubelin, G (2023–), *I Catch Killers Presents: Breaking Badness* [Audio podcast], NewsCast/True Crime Australia.

Maslow, AH (1968), *Toward a Psychology of Being* (2nd ed), Van Nostrand.

Rogers, CR (1961), *On Becoming a Person: A Therapist's View of Psychotherapy*, Houghton Mifflin.

Rosenthal, R, & Jacobson, L (1968), *Pygmalion in the Classroom, Holt*, Rinehart & Winston.

Whitfeld, A (2025), 'Inmate awarded PHD for prison garden design', ABC Radio National.

Chapter 5

Barrett, LF (2017), *How Emotions Are Made: The Secret Life of the Brain*, Houghton Mifflin Harcourt.

Bergquist, S (2025), *The Stress Paradox: Why You Need Stress to Live Longer, Healthier, and Happier*, HarperOne.

Gómez-Pinilla, F, & Gómez, AG (2011), 'The influence of dietary factors in central nervous system plasticity and injury recovery', *PM&R*, 3(6 Suppl 1), S111–S116.

Li, J, Kaltiainen, J, & Hakanen, JJ (2024), 'Job boredom as an antecedent of four states of mental health: Life satisfaction, positive functioning, anxiety, and depression symptoms among young employees—a latent change score approach', *BMC Public Health*, 24, 907.

Pickersgill, J, et al (2022), 'The combined influence of exercise, diet, and sleep on neuroplasticity', *Frontiers in Psychology*, 13, 831819.

Pope, A (1733–1734), *An essay on man: Epistle II*.

Raffaelli, Q, Mills, C, & Christoff, K (2018), 'The knowns and unknowns of boredom: A review of the literature', *Experimental Brain Research*, 236(9), 2451–2462.

Sanaeifar, M, et al (2024), 'Beneficial effects of physical exercise on cognitive-behavioral impairments and brain-derived neurotrophic factor alteration in the limbic system induced by neurodegeneration', *Experimental Gerontology*, 195, 112539.

Travers, M (2025), '3 ways the stress paradox fuels personal growth', *Forbes*.

Walker, MP (2009), 'The role of sleep in cognition and emotion', *Annals of the New York Academy of Sciences*, 1156(1), 168–197.

Yaribeygi, H, et al (2017), 'The impact of stress on body function: A review', *EXCLI Journal*, 16, 1057–1072.

Chapter 6

Cokley, KO (ed) (2022), *The Impostor Phenomenon: Psychological Research, Theory, and Interventions*, American Psychological Association.

Cokley, KO (guest) & Vedantam, S (host) (2021), 'The psychology of self-doubt', *Hidden Brain* [Audio podcast].

Crum AJ, et al (2017), 'The role of stress mindset in shaping cognitive, emotional, and physiological responses to challenging and threatening stress', *Anxiety Stress Coping*, 30(4), 379–395.

Crum, AJ, Salovey, P, & Achor, S (2013), 'Rethinking stress: The role of mindsets in determining the stress response', *Journal of Personality and Social Psychology*, 104(4), 716–733.

Dweck, CS (2008), 'Can personality be changed? The role of beliefs in personality and change', *Current Directions in Psychological Science*, 17(6), 391–394.

Heen, S, & Stone, D (2014), *Thanks for the Feedback: The Science and Art of Receiving Feedback Well*, Viking.

Kudesia, RS (2019), 'Mindfulness as metacognitive practice', *Academy of Management Review*, 44(2), 405–423.

Pychyl, TA (2013), *Solving the Procrastination Puzzle: A Concise Guide to Strategies for Change*, TarcherPerigee.

Sirois, FM, & Pychyl, TA (2013), 'Procrastination and the priority of short-term mood regulation: Consequences for future self', *Social and Personality Psychology Compass*, 7(2), 115–127.

Chapter 7

Blank, S (2013), 'Why the lean startup changes everything', *Harvard Business Review*, 91(5), 63–72.

Diamond, DM, et al (2007), 'The temporal dynamics model of emotional memory processing: A synthesis on the neurobiological basis of stress-induced amnesia, flashbulb and traumatic memories, and the Yerkes–Dodson law', *Neural Plasticity*, 2007, 60803.

Ellis, S, & Brown, M (2017), *Hacking growth: How Today's Fastest-Growing Companies Drive Breakout Success*, Crown Business.

Nahum-Shani, I, et al (2018), 'Just-in-time adaptive interventions (JITAIs) in mobile health: Key components and design principles for ongoing health behavior support', *Annals of Behavioral Medicine*, 52(6), 446–462.

Yerkes, RM, & Dodson, JD (1908), 'The relation of strength of stimulus to rapidity of habit formation', *Journal of Comparative Neurology & Psychology*, 18, 459–482.

Chapter 8

Ackoff, RL (1989), 'From data to wisdom', *Journal of Applied Systems Analysis*, 16, 3–9.

Barrett, LF (2017), *How Emotions are Made: The Secret Life of the Brain*, Houghton Mifflin Harcourt.

Deci, EL, & Ryan, RM (1985), *Intrinsic Motivation and Self-Determination in Human Behavior*, Plenum Press.

Di Stefano, G, et al (2014), 'Learning by thinking: How reflection aids performance', *Administrative Science Quarterly*, 59(2), 193–224.

Goleman, D (1988), 'Erikson, in his own old age, expands his view of life', *The New York Times*.

Heen, S, & Stone, D (2014), *Thanks for the Feedback: The Science and Art of Receiving Feedback Well*, Viking.

Kudesia, RS (2019), 'Mindfulness as metacognitive practice', *The Academy of Management Review*, 44(2), 405–423.

Ryan, RM, & Deci, EL (2000), 'Self-determination theory and the facilitation of intrinsic motivation, social development, and well-being', *American Psychologist*, 55(1), 68–78.

Chapter 9

Bandura, A (1997), *Self-Efficacy: The Exercise of Control*, W. H. Freeman.

Edmondson, A (1999), 'Psychological safety and learning behavior in work teams', *Administrative Science Quarterly*, 44(2), 350–383.

Edmondson, A (2011), 'Strategies for learning from failure', *Harvard Business Review*, 89(4), 48–55.

Eisenberger, NI, Lieberman, MD & Williams, KD (2003), 'Does rejection hurt? An fMRI study of social exclusion', *Science*, 302(56432), 290–292.

Kapur, M (2008), 'Productive failure', *Cognition and Instruction*, 26(3), 379–424.

Kapur, M (2016), 'Examining productive failure, productive success, unproductive failure, and unproductive success in learning', *Educational Psychologist*, 51(2), 1–11.

Neff, KD (2016), 'The self-compassion scale is a valid and theoretically coherent measure of self-compassion', *Mindfulness*, 7(1), 264–274.

Chapter 10

American Psychological Association (2019), *Clinical Practice Guideline for the Treatment of Depression across Three Age Cohorts*, American Psychological Association.

Cuijpers, P, et al (2016), 'Personalized psychotherapy for adult depression: A meta-analytic review', *Behavior Therapy*, 47(6), 966–980.

Kahneman, D, & Tversky, A (1979), 'Prospect theory: An analysis of decision under risk,' *Econometrica*, 47(2), 263–291.

Lilienfeld, SO, et al (2015), Science–practice gap', *The Encyclopedia of Clinical Psychology*.

Norcross, JC, & Wampold, BE (2011), 'Evidence-based therapy relationships: Research conclusions and clinical practices', *Psychotherapy (Chic)*, 48(1), 98–102.

Seneca (2015), *Letters from a Stoic* (R. Campbell, trans), Penguin Classics.

Chapter 11

Bakker, AB, & Demerouti, E (2007), 'The job demands–resources model: State of the art', *Journal of Managerial Psychology*, 22(3), 309–328.

Coyle, D (2018), *The Culture Code: The Secret of Highly Successful Groups*, Random House.

Deci, EL, & Ryan, RM (1985), *Intrinsic Motivation and Self-Determination in Human Behavior*, Plenum Press.

Edmondson, A (1999), 'Psychological safety and learning behavior in work teams', *Administrative Science Quarterly*, 44(2), 350–383.

Edmondson, AC (2018), *The Fearless Organization: Creating Psychological Safety in the Workplace for Learning, Innovation, and Growth*, John Wiley & Sons.

Fleming, W (2024), 'Employee well-being outcomes from individual-level mental health interventions: Cross-sectional evidence from the United Kingdom', *Industrial Relations Journal*, 55(2), 162–182.

Isoard-Gautheur, S, et al (2015), 'Development of burnout perceptions during adolescence among high-level athletes: A developmental and gendered perspective', *Journal of Sport & Exercise Psychology*, 37(4), 436–448.

Jones D, Molitor D, Reif J (2019), 'What do workplace wellness programs do? Evidence from the Illinois Workplace Wellness study', *Quarterly Journal of Economics*, 134(4), 1747–1791.

Kahn, WA (1990), 'Psychological conditions of personal engagement and disengagement at work', *Academy of Management Journal*, 33(4), 692–724.

Maslach, C, Schaufeli, WB, & Leiter, MP (2001), 'Job burnout', *Annual Review of Psychology*, 52, 397–422.

Newman, A, Donohue, R, & Eva, N (2017), 'Psychological safety: A systematic review of the literature', *Human Resource Management Review*, 27(3), 521–535.

Pink, DH (2009), *Drive: The Surprising Truth about What Motivates Us*, Riverhead Hardcover.

Reardon, C (2023), 'The mental health crisis in sports: The perfect storm of contemporary factors', *The Journal of Athletic Training*, 58(9), 677–680.

Ryan, RM, & Deci, EL (2000), 'Self-determination theory and the facilitation of intrinsic motivation, social development, and well-being', *American Psychologist*, 55(1), 68–78.

Smith, RE, Smoll, FL & Cumming SP (2007), 'Effects of a motivational climate intervention for coaches on young athletes' sport performance anxiety', *Journal of Sport & Exercise Psychology*, 29(1), 39–59.

World Economic Forum (2025), *Future of Jobs Report 2025*, World Economic Forum.

Wrzesniewski, A, et al (1997), 'Jobs, careers, and callings: People's relations to their work', *Journal of Research in Personality*, 31(1), 21–33.

Chapter 12

Fishbach, A, & Woolley, K (2022), The structure of intrinsic motivation', *Annual Review Organizational Psychology and Organizational Behavior*, 9, 339–363.

Grupe, DW, & Nitschke, JB (2013), Uncertainty and anticipation in anxiety: An integrated neurobiological and psychological perspective', *Nature Reviews Neuroscience*, 14(7), 488–501.

Ibarra, H, (2015), *Act Like a Leader, Think Like a Leader*, Harvard Business Review Press.

Kidd, C, & Hayden, BY (2015), 'The psychology and neuroscience of curiosity', *Neuron*, 88(3), 449–460.

Muthukrishna, M, & Henrich, J (2016), 'Innovation in the collective brain', *Philosophical Transactions of the Royal Society B*, 371(1690).

Yeager, DS, & Dweck, CS (2012), 'Mindsets that promote resilience: When students believe that personal characteristics can be developed', *Educational Psychologist*, 47(4), 302–314.

About the author

Tamsin Simounds applies the science of human growth to how we live, work and build careers.

She spent a decade in medical imaging, corporate healthcare leadership and organisational development, before shifting her career to spend the last decade coaching hundreds of executives and founders navigating growth, pressure and transformation. Along the way, she immersed herself in the science of behaviour change, studying the fields of applied psychology and neuroscience deeply and extensively.

She's lived it. She's learned it. She's taught it.

That convergent experience led her to create the Experiment Mindset Method—a practical, brain-aligned approach to change that bridges the gap between what people know and what they consistently do.

She has advised leaders across big banks, fast-growth startups and corporate organisations, and continues to speak and run workshops for professional audiences across Australia. Her work has been featured in *Smart Company*, *Thrive Global* and *Women's Agenda*.

Through her work and research, Tamsin has found that high-performance cultures burn people out, advocating instead for high personal growth cultures—environments where the experiment mindset can thrive, and where performance and wellbeing strengthen each other rather than compete.

Tamsin is also the founder of JumpProof, an Australian activewear startup developing absorbent technology to support women managing bladder symptoms during exercise. She's built it using the very principles of experimentation that she teaches.

She lives on a small farm in regional South Australia with her husband and two sons, where the Adelaide Hills meet the Fleurieu Peninsula, with more animals than is strictly reasonable. She practises what she teaches: building an ambitious life without losing herself in the process.

Learn more and connect with Tamsin at:
tamsinsimounds.com
linkedin.com/in/tamsinsimounds/
Instagram @tamsinsimounds

Acknowledgements

No meaningful experiment is run alone. This book exists because of the people who expanded my thinking, sustained my energy, and challenged me to grow when it would have been easier to stay the same.

To Jordon Lott, my Commissioning Editor at Wiley. Your email asking whether I had ever considered writing a book remains one of the best I've ever received. I had considered writing a book, but it may have been a decade or so away without that nudge. The moment I wrote the outline, I knew it was the right book at the right time—and it would not exist without you. Thank you, and thank you to the wider Wiley team for bringing it to life with such care and professionalism.

To Stacey Packer, you've been very patient with me. You could see the value in The Experiment Mindset approach and my potential to turn it into a book, years before I could. Thanks for sticking with me, for reading early drafts, and for keeping me steady during the rollercoaster that was writing it.

To Dr Michael Filosi, I chose you to read over my manuscript before it was finalised because I knew you'd be a tough but fair critic. You were generous with your time, care and rigorous feedback. The book is better because of it.

To every client and organisation that I've worked with over the past decade of my coaching and consulting career. I've learnt as much from you as you have from me. Your trust, challenges, and stories shaped and sharpened this work. Some of you may recognise yourselves in the client stories, and I hope you enjoy knowing that your stories are helping others.

To Chloe McLeod, Taimi Allan, James Galdes and James Begley—I feel incredibly lucky to collaborate with minds like yours. Thank you for your generosity and your contribution to this book.

To the researchers and thinkers who dedicate their lives to understanding the brain and human behaviour—I'm standing on your shoulders. Your work runs through these pages in both visible and invisible ways.

To the Medical Imaging company I began my career with, you created the work environment that helped me grow up professionally and gave me every opportunity to stretch and progress. I look back at my time working there very fondly and I'm thankful for all of the opportunities. Special thanks to the OG Area Manager team, we learned a lot together. And to the boss, Jeff Martin, who encouraged me to stick with it, made sure I was supported, and kept creating opportunities for career growth even as I had my babies. You're still cheering me on. Every emerging leader deserves a boss like you.

To Alistair Horscroft and The Mind Academy. Deciding to head to Noosa with a baby in tow to complete the Diploma of Modern Psychology course remains one of the bravest and best things I've done for my life. It stretched me, challenged me, changed me, and opened up my perspective on what's possible. It also gave me a toolkit that has allowed me to help hundreds of others. Al, you remain one of my great mentors. You've never been afraid to call me out or stretch my thinking and I'm grateful for that.

To Dean Evans, when I wanted to step on to a new path, you reached down, took my hand, and pulled me up. Thank you for believing in me.

To the Loxton High School—a public school in a small country town that punches well above its weight. Thank you to the teachers who supported me, offering not just education but genuine care, and thanks to the legendary class of '03.

To my high school friends, who have loved me through every version of myself, even the messy ones.

To the friends and family who have checked in along the way to see how the book was going, and cheered me on in the background, thank you for being there.

To my Dad, thanks for allowing me to tell my part of your story in hope that it can help others. It's been a tough ride at times, but the opportunities you created and supported helped lead me here.

To Mum, you put yourself second, third and fourth for so many years. I hope seeing what I've been able to build because of the foundation you laid—all the driving me around and tearing your hair out—gives you some relief. When I called to say I was moving back home because I was homesick, you didn't let me shrink my world, you moved to Adelaide instead. Huge. Thank you. I hope this book inspires you to keep experimenting.

To my big brother, Ben. You're the first person I call for the big career conversations, and you were one of the first people I trusted to run your eyes over the book. Your honesty and support mean more than you know. I hope this book makes you proud.

To Rosalie, I hit the mother-in-law jackpot. Thanks for your endless support, your help with pickups and drop offs, and for the mid-week family dinners while I wrote.

To my boys. I can run big experiments because I have big support at home.

To my husband, Dan. You believe in me in a way that no one ever has. You're not worried about me failing, and you've never tried to keep me small to keep me safe. You back me all the way in, and you look at me as if it's obvious that what I do will be a success. There's so much magic in that, and it's why my life cracked open when you entered it. My relatively last-minute plan to write a book in 2025 when our lives were already quite full, meant that you needed to pick up a lot of pieces. You work so hard to provide the stability that makes chasing my dreams possible. I could write all day and not express my love and thanks enough.

To Flynn and Charlie, my life's greatest joy and my greatest teachers. It's because of you that I'm driven to be my absolute best. You're funny, wise, kind and clever, and I hope that your lives are full of the most wonderous experiments, knowing that I'm right here to support you every step of the way.

Our beautiful, loyal 14-year-old border collie Nahla laid in the office next to me as I wrote every word of this book. She sadly passed before it was published. I'll always remember the love, comfort, and company she brought me over these months of writing.

And finally, to you, dear reader—thank you for your curiosity, your courage and your willingness to grow, and thank you for spending your precious time reading these pages. The world needs more people prepared to experiment their way to a better future. Now it's your turn.